Reach Up

By Vonda Kay Van Dyke

That Girl in Your Mirror
Dear Vonda Kay
Reach Up

Reach Up

Vonda Kay Van Dyke

FLEMING H. REVELL COMPANY
OLD TAPPAN, NEW JERSEY

Scripture references identified *KJV* are from the *King James Version of the Bible.*

Scripture references identified *LNT* are from *Living New Testament* by Kenneth N. Taylor, published by Tyndale House Publishers.

Scripture references identified *LL* are from *Living Letters* by Kenneth N. Taylor, published by Tyndale House Publishers.

Scripture references identified *TEV* are from the *Today's English Version of the New Testament.* Copyright © American Bible Society 1966.

Acknowledgment is made for use of the following songs: "Happiness" (Kurt Kaiser). Copyright © 1970 by Word, Incorporated. Used by permission. "Patches of Sunlight" (Vonda Kay Van Dyke). Copyright © 1971 by Word, Incorporated. Used by permission. "Reach Up" (Van Dyke-Gosh). Copyright © 1969 by Sacred Songs (A Division of Word, Incorporated). Used by permission.

No love, no friendship can ever cross the path of our destiny without leaving some mark upon it forever.

MAURIAC

This book is dedicated to each of you who has meant so much to me.

Contents

Preface

Once upon a time, like a few years before yesterday, for twelve brief shining months I was Miss America. During that very special year, out of a full and grateful heart, I wrote a book "from one very special girl," me, "to another very special girl," you, giving my best advice about *That Girl in Your Mirror* and how to bring out the unique beauty deep down in every one of you. Then I wrote another to answer some of the questions you had addressed during my reign to *Dear Vonda Kay*. Your response to these efforts and to me personally when we've met have been so terrific that our friendship and my real concern for you have continued to grow and deepen since I passed on my crown.

I'd like to tell you what I've learned by sharing with you some of my own experiences. These are things I've learned by living them.

I am going to try, between these covers, to give you my best, to use ink and paper to share some of the experiences from my personal record so that you can be sure it's more than advice. In that once-upon-a-time most of what I knew had been taught to me, or I had acquired it from other people. One of the conditions of youth seems to be that everyone is trying to "make something of us." What that something is depends on who's giving the advice—parent, teacher, advertiser, friend, critic. Many young people respond in one of two ways. They conform. Or they rebel. Both these paths lead to failure— failure to live creatively and constructively, failure to become what you alone can be, failure to make the most out of your life. But once you have begun to question, and the teen-ager who isn't questioning isn't thinking, then it's true that it often requires better judgment to separate the good advice from the bad than is necessary in making your own decisions. When I had really grown up enough to question, a middle path opened for me, a way in which we can make our own decision, make of ourselves not a stagnant something, but an exciting, growing someone, a real person. This way leads to success and wholeness. It is the way I want to share with you.

Above all I want to tell you about my philosophy of life and how it gives me that something extra, something firm that I can stand on no matter what is happening in the world around me. I want to show you how it has worked in helping me set goals, overcome problems, and given me the courage to welcome the changes and challenges we all face.

Together we'll hold that mirror up to life and I'll try to tell it like it is—for me. For I myself am looking in a different mirror now. I don't see the image of Miss America in it any more. Or any other man-made image. I see a real, evolving person, the someone I think God wants each of us to become, one who is free to love and create and share and experience and enjoy.

Does this mean I've changed?

Recently I went back to the Miss America Pageant in Atlantic City to help celebrate the pageant's Golden Anniversary. Bert Parks, the Emcee who has sung "There she is . . ." to many a winner, including me, said that the Miss America crown has such enormous public appeal because it represents the biggest Cinderella story we have in real life. In a split second one hometown girl out of some seventy-thousand other hometown girls realizes the dream of them all and becomes a queen for one year. Well, the end of Cinderella's story is known to all of us. As in all good fairy tales she obviously marries the prince "and lives happily ever after."

But in real life what happens to Cinderella after the ball is over?

So many people wondered if the Miss America year would "change our Vonda Kay" that a dear friend of mine, Sandy Gibbons, who's involved in TV and radio in my hometown, Phoenix, sent me a copy of his answer. Here's what he said:

Good evening . . . tonight, a very interesting subject and one that has been at one time or other close to our hearts. It concerns the reigning Miss America, and the all too brief moments left in this tenuous grasp on the hearts of Americans. Will she return home that same, sweet, unsophisticated girl we cheered and cried on to a crown? Or will she return a conquering hero without a throne, a confused castoff from the commercial capriciousness of big business thrown into a world shorn of its glamour and open hearts? Probably, if she was still a sweet, unsophisticated girl such would be the case. But our Vonda is a girl who can now accept things as they are. . . . You bet she'll be different and in a way that many of us will never achieve! In one instant she was given a crown, a scepter, and a kingdom to dominate. Has Vonda changed? Of course, she's changed . . . into a wonderful woman touched by the hand of God and the will of His people. She's still a trouper . . . the stage is just a little wider.

Reading this over I have to ask myself, "Have I changed?" I hope so. I hope I've grown a little toward this high goal my friend held up for me.

I can only speak for myself but when this queen became a commoner overnight she found herself in a wonderful world of opportunity—the same normal American world we all live in—and it was up to her to make something of it. Being Miss "A" had given her some advantages, and some disadvantages, as you'll see, but so does being a campus homecoming queen, a state or local queen, a cheerleader, a football hero. We have to profit by our opportunities and our successes as well as by our failures. We'll talk about that, too, because every experience rounds and shapes us into a more complete person if we are open and allow the improvement to be made.

I now have the wider stage Sandy spoke of; among other things, I have become a professional singer. (I now even wear false eyelashes at times!) And in my new world, far from losing anything, my philosophy of life has shown me how to make gains. I've learned a confidence I didn't know I lacked, a humility I didn't know I needed. In learning to care about an audience I've learned to care more about people in general —and you in particular.

And if I've changed—well, so have you.

During my Miss America year I did a lot of growing up, traveling to far distant places, meeting and talking to a wide variety of people. In fact, I aged so rapidly that I got exactly twenty-one gray hairs. I'd never had one before and I've never gotten one since, but you can see that this particular crown and the image that it represented gave me a heavy sense of responsibility. And while I was doing my growing up, so, it seems to me, was young America. When I meet you now at rallies, or on personal appearances, or in church groups, I find you not only more open, more honest, but far more interested in the really important things of life than the young people I'd known before. You are more excited about the future, more aware of the big, wide world, more thoughtful about your place in it. That's why I feel we can talk now about things like ecology and women's lib instead of what to wear, about men and marriage instead of rules for dating, about all-round successful happy living instead of how to win a contest.

Dudley Dowell once wisely said: "It seems to me that the key to our future can be summed up in one word—adaptability. In a rapidly changing world it is often a matter of survival to change one's mind—one's attitude—one's way of thinking and doing things. Even when survival is not at issue, we should all know how to adjust to changed circumstances in order to capitalize on new opportunities.

The philosophy of life I've found is one thing that has *not* changed. When I commenced my Miss America year I said my Bible was the most important book I owned. It still is. I hope I can show you why. I also said my highest goal was to "live up to my Christian testimony." This was one of my more noble statements and I was sincere at the time, but as I look back from the real adult world I've wished so many times I had changed that one. Because I fail so many times, in so many ways, to be "Christ's example on earth," because I probably always will, I wish I'd had the humility to add the little word "try."

For me, two of the most important words I know are short. Both have only three letters. The first is *God*. The second is *try*. And I think what the first expects of us is the second. *God* expects us to *try*.

When I ended my Miss America year I said I was not stepping down. I was "stepping up—

to a new life,
a new challenge!"

This has proven true.

Now, with God's help, I'll try to hold a mirror up to those challenges, to that new life, so we can step up—together.

I wish to thank Elaine St. Johns for her help with this book. Also, I would like to thank again the wonderful people of the Fleming H. Revell Company for their efforts, encouragement and deepening friendship.

Reach Up

It's important that we learn when we're young to reach out and gather up all the opportunities that come our way. We need to reach out into the world around us, gathering and storing all the knowledge available to us, and we need to reach out and share with others.

I feel strongly that it's also important for us to reach up. By reaching up to God we can build our inner selves. Drawing from His love, help, and guidance, we can face the world with confidence, knowing "All things work together for the good of them that know God, to them who are called according to His purpose."

We know that all that happens to us is for our good if we are fitting into God's plans and loving Him.

1

Happiness Is . . .

Happiness can be defined as many *things* by many people, but one thing is for sure. It's what we want to *be*. It's the goal set for us by our Declaration of Independence.

Long before we cut our wisdom teeth we have planted in our minds our All-American right to "the pursuit of happiness." And our hearts agree. Our hearts take an even bigger leap. We have, it says, the right to catch up with it. As kids that can be simple: a soft puppy, an "A" in new math, hitting a home run with bases loaded, a Christmas tree surrounded by our dreams all tied up with bows on top, a vacation meadow full of butterflies or a beach dotted with sea shells—and we're where it's at.

For adults happiness seems a lot more complicated.

As horizons widen, as we are tugged this way and that by conflicting desires, conflicting ideas, conflicting promises as to what and where the Good Life is, simplicity disappears under mountains of verbal confetti. Our guiding compass swings to the magnetic cry of a thousand tempting choices. "This way to the Big Show. Follow me! Try me! Taste me . . . drink me . . . buy me . . ." until the bewildered seeker feels a bit like Alice in Wonderland, sampling first this, then that, only to find the goal blurred as he spins around in a circle of confusion.

If you and I are to pursue happiness, and are to actually find it and keep it, we should be very clear about what it really is for each of us.

I've had to think that out for myself because I'm often accused of happiness. Sometimes it appears that I've been caught stealing a rainbow, and I'm challenged to explain how I got my hands on the thing.

"Oh, you're so happy," someone will say. "What are you so happy about?"

Well, happiness, for me isn't chasing rainbows and trying to lock them in my dresser drawer. But it is being sensitive and aware enough to enjoy it when it happens. It isn't doing or having what someone else thinks is valuable. It's doing my own thing and feeling right with the world about it. It's made up of little things that make me feel warm and glad; of bigger things that give me a glow of achievement and satisfaction; of great things that sing inside with a stirring of peace and comfort and joy.

I feel I'm really where it's at when all these things add up to a loving creative relationship to all of life—people, places, activities, and the wonders in the world around me. So, when someone asks me what I'm so happy about I say that I'm happy about life, about all the things that turn me on:

The hot fudge sundae at the end of a diet
Chocolate cake and milk for breakfast
A cherry soda with chocolate ice cream
When one of my puppies decides to use the paper instead of the floor
Feeling wind and spray and sun when I'm water-skiing
Listening to the silence of an audience when I'm singing a soft ballad
Discovering beautiful things and beautiful people
Flying above the clouds
Snorkling—seeing a live lobster on the ocean floor, multicolored fish, and an old wrecked ship
Walking into a roomful of people, saying "Hi" to strangers, leaving saying "Good-by" to friends

Showing appreciation and being appreciated
Knowing someone cares
Reaching the goal I thought was impossible
Taking all I can from life, but *giving* it just as much or more

Along with being happy I'm also accused of smiling a lot. Well, when I'm glad inside, it turns on a smile outside. What else? It's a natural reaction, like giggling when you're tickled, or having a temperature of 98.6° when you're healthy. Anyone can take his own "turn-on" temperature in the nearest mirror.

It seems sad to me that kids appear to find so much to smile about, and some adults so little. Of course the young can still see what Robert Louis Stevenson saw when he wrote *A Child's Garden of Verses:* "The world is so full of a number of things, I'm sure we should all be as happy as kings." Corny? Perhaps, but when we get too sophisticated to see those "things" we're not progressing, we're regressing. True, as we grow older we have more and bigger problems and challenges to face. But if we sacrifice our awareness of and sensitivity to the soft puppy, the butterflies in the meadow, the taste of cold watermelon on a hot day to what the adult world considers really important we've lost something of infinite value. Our horizon will narrow instead of widen. And our chance of happiness will be diminished.

If we are clear about what happiness really is we can keep our original gift of appreciation and wonder. Then, in the face of the bigger challenges, we can add to it the mature ability to "turn on" in the pursuit of excellence.

I've found that I get that glow of achievement and satisfaction, when I can say, "I'm happy about my goals and ambitions, who I am, and what I'm doing right now." With all this working for me I can smile a different kind of smile.

Smiling from the Inside

I can honestly say that I smile from the inside when I know I've done my best and tried my hardest; made something work; found a solution to a problem by trial and error.

Many people, including Webster's Dictionary, say that among other definitions happiness reflects good luck. Not in my mirror it doesn't. In my experience you make your own luck.

As a little girl I went each fall with my family to the state fair. One year I was fascinated by a booth where you threw your nickel at a flat plate. If it stayed on the plate, you got a fluffy live baby duck. If it rolled off, the man got your nickel. While we watched, a lot of grown-ups lost a lot of nickels. But the man didn't lose a single duckling. Nevertheless I announced firmly to my parents that next year I would win a duck. Starting that very night I set a flat plate in the kitchen and began throwing nickels at it. Over the weeks I threw from different distances and different angles. I learned to put a little spin on the nickel so it would land flat and not roll.

The next November I went straight to that booth and, when it came my turn, confidently took out my nickel, threw it on the plate, and there it stayed. The man saw that I had done it on my first try so he said, "Goodness, that was really luck. If you can do it again I'll give you two more ducks." So, only smiling on the inside, I missed on the second try, but with my third nickel I did it again and went home with three cuddly ducks.

Since then I've proved over and over to myself that, while no one can win 'em all, the more effort I've put into something the better I've felt about me and the greater my chances of being lucky.

"When I've Been Discouraged Without Giving Up . . ."

For me one of the handicaps of having been Miss America was that, although for thirty-five years Pageant contestants have been judged as much on talent, intellect, and personality as on appearance, there still vibrate over Atlantic City echoes from a half-century ago when Miss America received her crown wearing nothing but a smile and a swimsuit.

Dedicated pageant officials have worked very hard to transform the image of Miss America into what it is today and have stressed the fact that it is a scholarship pageant for the American girl who seeks to expand her horizons. Still, I had the feeling that no matter what I accomplished some people thought my talent bound to remain amateur and my profession bound to remain "ex-beauty queen."

A major challenge in becoming a professional singer was to sing so well that an audience would be just as interested in listening to me as in looking at me. Every normal woman wants to be as pretty as possible and to be admired. But she also knows that to be successful she can't be "only" pretty, and she must achieve admiration for something beside her looks.

A little over a year ago, I thought I'd met that challenge. Dick Shack, head of the Miami office of the Agency for Performing Arts and the man who manages my career, had booked me for my first major extended engagement in Houston, Texas. Dick produced a convention show in Freeport and put me on the show in order to give me an opportunity to break in the new act. The audience reaction was great and I really felt like a professional singer. After the show, however, people kept coming up saying, "Gee, you're so pretty." "You look so beautiful." Not one of them said I had sung well. Mr. Shack, who not only helped me start but helped to guide and encourage my career, assured me that the reaction to my appearance rather than my vocal ability was only because the convention group were people in the cosmetic industry. I was discouraged and felt he was just trying to excuse the situation away. But I just couldn't give up.

After closing my two-week engagement, I was convinced I was on the right track when I received a lovely letter from the manager of the Shamrock Hilton Hotel saying how much he had enjoyed the act and that he was certain that I would go a long way.

Exactly one year later, Dick booked me on another show that he was producing in Freeport. The reaction to this one was exactly what I had been hoping for. Everyone made comments like, "We really enjoyed your show" and "I loved your voice." There were none of the compromising comments about my being pretty. I felt I had come a long way and that this was one of the happiest moments I ever had.

When I Search for and Find Something Interesting in What Seemed an Uninteresting Person . . .

Happiness is certainly being with people you enjoy, so obviously the more people you can enjoy the happier you'll be.

I used to find some people dull and to be bored is to be very unhappy. Then one night before we were Dr. and Mrs. C. Andrew Laird, Andy and I went to a party. Much to my surprise I found all the men off in one corner and all the women clustered around the fireplace. What to do? Obviously go with the women, I said to myself. See what happens. What happened was a lot of in-talk about diaper rash (which left me out), soap operas (I was still attending classes at UCLA by daylight), a new biodegradeable detergent for dishwashers (I had yet to encounter my first of either). I couldn't very well join the men, and I couldn't seem to get with the ladies either, so I tuned out, turned off, and just sat being miserable. Perhaps I wasn't a great success at the party, but I didn't think the young couples very groovy either.

Later I got to thinking. One of the great advantages of my Miss America year was that I met a lot of people and made a lot of friends. The pace was fast and exciting—and all the lovely people took such an interest in *me*. Obviously under the new ground rules if I wanted to say "Hi" to strangers and "Goodbye" to friends I had to make a mental change. I had to find a way to be interested in *them* no matter what. So I began to play a game with myself.

I must *learn* something from everyone I meet!

Everyone, I decided, had something to say, or knew something I didn't know. The game was to uncover it. With apparently dull or very shy people I sometimes had to stay with it a long time. It was kind of like the situation Jacob found himself in in the Old Testament times, when he wrestled with an angel all night beside the Jabbok brook insisting, "I will not let thee go, except thou bless me" (Genesis 32:26 KJV). Jacob finally got his blessing. So I'd hang on, saying mentally, "you're going to come up with something sometime. I won't let you go until you do." And, sure enough, they always did.

To find that there are, in truth, no uninteresting people has proven a real blessing because I can't think of anyone anymore that I don't enjoy being with.

Most definitely I can say, *"I get that inner glow from learning."*

For me this is one of the most exciting facets of happiness. I think life can be very unexciting if you don't learn something every day. Too often we limit ourselves by separating learning from life. We think we "learn" only when we're young, or from books, or in school. But I find an immense satisfaction in constantly finding out new things about me as well as other people, and about the world around me. If we are thoroughly alive and alert everything we do can result in learning. Even small personal discoveries can be just as exciting as understanding Einstein's earth-shaking disclosure that $E = mc^2$.

It's great to discover that in art we are free to like whatever we want to.

It was fascinating to discover from my first dishwasher that if I put in regular soap I could manufacture a roomful of suds.

Learning that a blade of grass really does have the power to grow through asphalt was not only an adventure but really meaningful. True, I had been taught the fact in school, but it didn't do a thing for me until I saw it happen.

The saga of the blade of grass began not long ago just after the alley behind our house was paved. One day I noticed this little brown point pushing right through the asphalt. It was bent from the struggle but once it broke through into the light it grew straight and tall as if it was trying to reach up and touch the sun. With each dawn it looked greener and more healthy until it was a very proper blade of grass indeed. I had never watched such a small, seemingly insignificant thing so closely before, and the courage and determination of that lone blade delighted me. Then suddenly I got the message, and it didn't seem insignificant at all. I thought, "Well, it's like anything else." Nothing is impossible if you really try. If that little thing can make its way right through asphalt, I can certainly make my way through my problems.

I found myself caring very much about that blade of grass. I really wanted it to make good. Every time my husband came in the driveway I'd say, "Don't run over the blade of grass!" Caring made me want to protect it. Again I got the message. I could better understand and appreciate all the people—my wonderful parents, my kind teachers, relatives, and friends—everyone who had cared enough to protect me, to give me the chance to grow up and become strong and stand tall in the sun.

When Andy and I left for our vacation, I thought about the little green thing and wondered if it would survive. On our return there it was, sturdy and flourishing. But it wasn't alone anymore. There were other blades coming up all around it. I thought, Of course! If one person is reaching up, fighting to live for something, to accomplish something, and actually makes a breakthrough, it's bound to have an influence. There will be others interested in pursuing goals and climbing ladders who will see that it can be done, and they will reach up to achieve wider, more successful lives.

And if a person goes even further, pushing strongly toward the very best life, the life that has cause and meaning, that is truly worthwhile and gives the greatest happiness. Perhaps that could encourage others to reach higher still and lead them to the sunshine of a brand new day.

"New Kind of Happiness"

Last spring, after I did a show for the statewide 4-H Club Roundup at Texas A & M, one of the young people said to me, "Isn't it wonderful that you can be groovy and still believe in God." It was a great compliment but I couldn't quite accept it because, you see, I feel I can be really groovier *because* I believe in God.

When I tell people, "I'm happy about life, where I am, who I am, about what I'm doing right now, my goals, my ambition," and explain to them how I got that way, I know from my own experience that they can walk this same way to a happier, more successful life. But actually, I've saved the best for last. Because then I say, "Of course I'm happy because of my faith in God, too."

It is my faith that brings me that sense of joy, the kind of happiness that can swing me right out of this world. I can understand why King David, who has to be one of the most popular lyric writers of all time (the Psalms have been solid international hits for 3,000 years), used the line, "Make a joyful noise" unto God, in seven of his songs.

One of the goals I thought impossible and which I've reached in the last few years was to do religious albums for young people that would really swing to get across that "joyful noise." When I first mentioned it, the record people just laughed and said it wouldn't work. Then Word Records decided that the time was right for just this kind of music, but I'll admit that at first it shook up a few people.

Once in New York when I arrived for a recording session, there were eight or nine wild looking musicians in the studio complete with the far-out hair and the freaked-out clothes. As they ran through the music, they really were getting into it, really starting to groove. "Oh, yea man," they kept saying as they played.

When we started recording I was in the booth singing into my mike and the orchestra couldn't hear me. They had no idea that we were doing a religious song. On the playback when we reached the part where I mentioned Christ's name, they all jerked up and gasped.

"What was that, man? What was that? You mean this is a religious song? Man, I never heard a religious song like this!"

They were convinced that religious music was downbeat and

dreary. But the real message of the new contemporary religious music isn't really new at all. And it's not dreary. David wrote when he praised God a couple of thousand years before that: ". . . in thy presence is fulness of joy; at thy right hand there are pleasures for evermore" (Psalm 16:11 KJV). Christ Himself said that He had come into the world so that those who believed in Him "might have life, and that they might have it more abundantly" (John 10:10 KJV). He asked us to keep His commandments not to restrict our lives, but so that "my joy may be in you, and that your joy may be complete" (John 15:11 TEV).

The great message for modern man is that His promises are kept. And for today one of the best ways to say it is to sing it like now.

In learning to put a little bit more of me into everything, I've had the courage to write some songs that express my deep down feeling and to record them—one in my first album and three in my second release, *New Kind of Happiness.*

A song without music is, I'll admit, pretty much like a cherry soda without chocolate ice cream. There won't be the right "noise," but I hope the"joyful" feeling will come across.

The chorus of "Patches of Sunlight" that I wrote for my newest album should, I guess, be dedicated to one remarkable blade of grass, because surely its adventure provided the seed that grew into this song.

> You're walkin' in patches of sunlight,
> Why don't you begin—living in
> The daily radiance of knowing Him.
> Step out of the shadows
> That fall across your way
> And march into the sunshine
> Of a brand new day.

The title for the second album came from a snappy clap-along type song I wrote to express how relevant God seems to happiness in our lives today. In the three verses I tried to show what's missing if you don't know about Jesus Christ. They begin:

You're not with it/If you don't know Him . . .
You'll never belong/Until He becomes your friend . . .
You're not with it/If you haven't felt His love . . .
You won't be headin' for the heavenly home above

And in the chorus I tried to tell it like it is:

> Get with it, People,
> Don't wait too long.
> Just pick up the beat to
> A new kind of song.
> Clap your hands
> To a new kind of happiness.
> Try the life that's
> Always the best.

When we had finished these and the six other songs in recording sessions that ran late into the night, we still needed one more to complete the album. Over a cup of hot chocolate with Kurt Kaiser, the brilliant young conductor-composer who had just masterminded our session, we discussed ideas for the last song. I felt it had to be something special. "It should say that being a Christian is happy—fun," I said. "That you've always got Someone with you to help you. It's confidence. It's an addition to a person's life." I guess I was thinking of the 4-H Roundup when I added, "It should say that being a Christian is something extra and really groovy."

Kurt agreed, but where was the song? That night "Happiness" was born. I don't know how late Kurt worked, but first thing in the morning he called and, in his voice that was never meant to sing, he half recited the opening bars.

> Happiness is knowing that
> The Lord is by your side.
> Happiness is knowing that
> With you He will abide.
> Happiness is knowing that,
> No matter where you go,
> He can make it happen.
> I know 'cause He told me so . . .

Next day we recorded it in a "happy kid" style. I talked bits with drum solos, and when I sang for the voice track I was so tickled that I giggled. This added the inside feeling. When I came to the final line, "Happiness is knowing the Lord," I knew those five words really said it.

Jesus Himself established "the pursuit of happiness" as a Christian goal, but He went a lot further than Thomas Jefferson did. Christ told us exactly where it's at, and exactly how to catch up with it. Standing on a hill, talking to a great crowd of ordinary, trying people just like you and me, He taught them:

> "Happy are those who know they are
>   spiritually poor:
>   the Kingdom of heaven belongs to
>   them!
> "Happy are those who mourn:
>   God will comfort them!
> "Happy are the meek:
>   they will receive what God has promised!
> "Happy are those whose greatest desire
>   is to do what God requires:
>   God will satisfy them fully!
> "Happy are those who show mercy to
>   others:
>   God will show mercy to them!
> "Happy are the pure in heart:
>   they will see God!
> "Happy are those who work for peace
>   among men:
>   God will call them his sons!
> "Happy are those who suffer persecution
>   because they do what God requires:
>   the Kingdom of heaven belongs to
>   them!" (Matthew 5: 3-10, TEV)

And that's what Christian happiness is—a promise for now and for all eternity.

2

Your Future Is Now

One of the wonderful things that turned me on as a child was helping my Grandpa Arthur plant flowers and vegetables. I can remember my sense of awe when I realized that, by cupping my hands, I could hold the seeds of an entire garden. Or forest.

The seeds, Grandpa explained, were *potential*.

Recently I did a series of high-school assemblies in the northern part of the country and talked to some ten thousand young people. I felt that same sense of awe when I realized that, packed in those audiences was such enormous potential, seeds of beauty and talent that promised wonderful growth for our future garden of man.

I was awed too by the magnificent challenge of the human condition. A petunia seed, if properly planted and cared for, has no choice but to grow into a mature petunia. It cannot decide to be a singing petunia or a sighing petunia, successful and worthwhile on the one hand or ineffectual and confused on the other. Can you imagine a petunia in search of meaning? But each individual in those audiences had the free will first to discover his unique potential, then to choose exactly how far he would develop it.

Unlike the seed, our lives unfold more like a voyage as we slip from the narrow headwaters of home into the wider stream of school, and finally into an ocean of infinite possibilities. Our freedom of choice is the rudder that guides our journey.

Throughout the teens, as we get into deeper water, acquire more right to make our own choices, we also become more aware of the hazards. There are rocks that can hang us up, rapids that can spin us off course. Stagnant ponds that keep us watching as the mainstream of life flows by. But we are well launched on a great adventure and we know it; we feel sure we can arrive at an exciting, meaningful destination *if* we make the right choices.

When I found myself facing those thousands of young people, knowing they were headed for the open sea, the first thing I wanted to tell them was the importance (not only for themselves but for those in the older generation who look to them and believe in them) of discovering their individual talents, and setting their individual goals.

On a recent tour of NASA our guide looked at our group, all of us in our twenties or younger, and said, "We're doing this for your generation." It's another way of saying that you and I are the future. They've found out that the moon isn't made of green cheese. What will we make of it?

So it seems very important to me to listen to your ideas and problems, to help you find your directions, construct your goals and build your philosophies, for many of the ideals and patterns you are setting as early as the teens will affect us all for the rest of our lives.

It is said that if a man doesn't know where he is going no wind is favorable to him. Finding that out is a major challenge in our early lives. History proves we're never too young to start.

By the age of fifteen Thomas Edison had learned to operate a telegraph instrument and he became an operator. By the age of twenty-one he obtained his first patent. In the next few years Edison worked on many of his numerous inventions.

James Watt was still in his twenties when he improved upon and perfected the steam engine. For years he diligently experimented and finally realized success.

Mme. Curie, the famous scientist, discovered her love of physics in high school. Although she married and had children she chose to develop her full potential. At thirty-six she had made such an outstanding contribution to the world that, along with her husband and another male scientist, she was awarded the Nobel prize.

Edna St. Vincent Millay started writing poetry in her very early teens, published her extraordinary *Renascence* at twenty-five, and won the Pulitzer prize at thirty-one.

So you can see that, we all need to be interested in the future, no matter which generation we belong to, because it is where we will spend the rest of our lives. The all important fact is that the future begins today. What we are today is the result of what we did with yesterday. What we do today will guide us into tomorrow. If today is not to our liking, if we hope for a better tomorrow, if we are uncertain or worried about the future, we have to get with it *now*. No matter what age we are, we *are* the Now generation.

So how do we go about it?

Find Your Own Particular Talent

Science has provided us with concrete proof of our individuality. When we realize that no two hairs on our head, no two thumbprints, or, for that matter, no two petunias are exactly alike, we can have complete confidence that each of us has a unique potential. This is not to say that there couldn't be two housewives or two teachers or two singers. We each have two thumbs. But the individual print will be uniquely our own.

We will begin to set our true self-image and worth if we can believe that whoever we are, some younger person thinks we are perfect; that certain work will never be done unless we do it; that someone would miss us if we were gone; that there is a place we alone can fill. These are good reasons for becoming a better person.

This doesn't mean that each of us has the talent to be a great inventor or scientist or the first woman president. Nor that we would want to be. It means, as St. Paul wrote, that "God has given each of us the ability to do certain things well" (Romans 12:6 LNT).

Few young people are as fortunate as the immortal Felix Mendelssohn who gave his first concert and began to compose at the age of nine. Or Edison who found his own thing just as he turned the teen corner. Or even Mme. Curie whose talent was outstanding in high school. For most of us these are the years to investigate and explore.

I understand that Conrad Hilton once gave some excellent advice. "Don't worry about what you haven't got in the way of talent," said the hotelman. "Find out what you *have*." He then told the story of a poor Greek who applied for a position in a bank in Athens. "Can you write?" he was asked. "Only my name," said the man. He didn't get the job so he borrowed money and traveled steerage to the United States, the Land of Opportunity. Years later an important Greek businessman held a press conference in his Wall Street offices. At the conclusion a reporter said, "You should write your memoirs." The gentleman smiled. "Impossible," he said. "I cannot write." The reporter was amazed. "Just think," he said, "how much further you'd have gone if you could." The Greek shook his head. "If I could write," he said, "I'd have been a janitor."

However little we may seem to start out with, whatever our handicaps, the objective is to find out what we *have*. This takes the confidence to believe in ourselves and the humility to be honest in our self-appraisal.

I can only tell it as it happened.

When I arrived in high school all I knew was that I'd probably go to college. My parents expected it of me and, more important, I expected it of myself. If my destination turned out to be house-wife, any special abilities I might discover and cultivate would only round out my full potential.

A lot of young people, and a lot of older people who prod and influence young people, are hung up on the question, "What are you *going* to do with your life?" The problem is that most of us don't know. If we spend our time worrying about what we are *going* to do, the end result is apt to be wishful thinking. "Wouldn't it be great to be an astronaut?" "I'd just love to be a model!" Wishful thinking has about the same relationship to definite ideals and goals as worry has to positive action. Neither produce any forward motion. As Alexander Wollcott once said, "Many of us spend half our time wishing for things we could have if we didn't spend half our time wishing." It's equally useless to spend half our time worrying about problems we could solve if we didn't spend half our time worrying about them. During the time spent worrying and wishing we're not alert to ideas, not concentrating on what we're doing *now*.

But what happens if you relax and say, "Let's see what unfolds if I take one step at a time," and then step out with purpose to do what's there to be done? If your direction isn't set in high school, well, why not take a general precollege course and get the best possible grades *now,* because you might want to go to college? Then as different interests and opportunities present themselves, you can explore them, too. Get moving. Get involved. Find out about you.

When I got to junior college I still didn't know where I was *going,* but I wasn't concerned about it. I'd found out a lot (and had a lot of fun) by entering into all the activities that appealed to me. In grade school I discovered that, while I liked sports, I was only an average athlete. I was great in competition though. I hit my first and last pair of home runs in a championship baseball game.

I had discovered you didn't have to be a carbon copy; you could make your own impression if you had the courage to be different. My mother was always in great demand as a piano player. Me, I wound up being the only girl to play tenor saxophone in the school band.

In high school my most surprising discovery was that I had an exceptionally loud voice. So cheerleading was a natural for me. Then, in my senior year, I entered the Junior Miss contest.

I didn't tell any of my friends about it because I certainly didn't think I qualified as "the ideal high-school girl." But since contestants were judged on talent, character, high school activities, scholastic achievement, personal ambition, citizenship, poise, and demeanor—all the things I believed made a well-rounded personality—I thought I'd surely know myself better if these qualities were evaluated by experts.

When I won I was amazed. But it was when I lost in the national contest in Mobile, Alabama, that I really learned something which has been of value ever since.

Potential Has to Be Cultivated

Too often the "talented child" in grammar school, the "most likely to succeed" in high school, the runner-up in a contest, have missed the mark because they lacked the stamina and determination to make the most of their potential. I got to know all the other girls in the top ten at Mobile and they were the greatest. But the winner was the one who had worked the hardest to develop what she had to start with.

In everything, whether it's developing a rounded personality, helping a child reach maturity, or working out a marriage happily, it seems to take time and patience and effort. I'd seen that, too, in Grandpa's garden. As with plants and flowers, so with us. Our first small shoots must be cared for and nourished. Whether we are cultivating a talent, reading about how to improve our personality, accepting a wedding band on our finger, or having a child, the more care and time we give it, the more weeding out of harmful things, the stronger and healthier the new growth will be. Sometimes the "least likely to succeed" work the hardest—and outdistance those with greater gifts.

All I had proven in winning those early contests was that whatever potential I had needed a lot more cultivation.

So there I was attending Phoenix College fully realizing that it would take time and patience and effort to *arrive,* but still not knowing where I was *going.* So I took inventory.

The first question was, Why was I there? Certainly I hadn't come to college for my "Mrs." degree. Nor as a status symbol. Nor because I couldn't think of anything better to do. I was there to prepare *now* for what the future might unfold. What if I never married? What if my husband died? I was looking for an academic vocation in which I could use my abilities to live a life both financially successful and personally satisfying.

I considered my natural abilities and talents as I knew them. Emerson said, "Each man has his own vocation. The talent is the call . . . he inclines to do something which is easy for him, and good when it is done." What did I like to do? When I won the state Junior Miss contest, the newspapers quoted me as saying I liked to cook, sew, sing and do my ventriloquist act. All true. But no way to a B.A.

I took some written tests which indicated a lot of interesting things, among them that I would be good at working with people. Well, I would certainly enjoy that. Coupled with the fact that I'd been appearing in public since I was six, liked to talk, and had a voice of goodly volume I thought, "Well, I'd major in speech." Mr. Emerson would approve. It would be easy for me. Education was the vehicle for making a profession of speech, so I took education.

I stepped out firmly and with purpose and made another discovery. I took an overload of subjects, carrying up to twenty-one units in one semester. I involved myself in everything on campus. Again I was a cheerleader. I was in several dramatic productions, including musicals like *The Boy Friend*. I sang in the choir. Off campus I had my first brush with the Miss America Pageant and got as far as first runner-up for Miss Phoenix. With all these outside activities I made better grades than I did at any other time in college because I pushed. I budgeted my time and made it work. My scholastic average and activities on campus won me a position on the college honor board. Furthermore, instead of taking the usual two years I was graduated in a year and a half.

The biggest thing I learned about myself in junior college was that the more I pushed the more I got done, and the better I did it.

After a semester at Northern Arizona University, I returned to Tempe, a town just outside of Phoenix. It was while attending Arizona State University that I got all excited about speech therapy, helping kids with speech defects (cleft palate and stuttering), attempting to show them how to speak so that they could be understood. Here I could get really involved and satisfy my ideal of service. In theory it was great. But I found out another thing. Tests and counselors are certainly helpful but they aren't infallible because there are facets in each of us that only experience brings to light. I was good working with people unless I got *too* involved with them. I had such sympathy for those kids that I forgot they were really happy because they were learning. I was so busy telling them how much I liked them and wanted them to improve and was so overwhelmed with sympathy that I didn't teach them anything to help them. I barely passed the course. It was the lowest grade I ever got in college.

Some form of early apprenticeship could save a lot of us from wasted time and disappointment later. The girl who thinks she wants to be a nurse should certainly do some volunteer hospital work before she dedicates herself to the long pull. She may have too much heart or too little stomach for the job. The same would apply to anyone who wants to be a doctor.

By the time I settled in Arizona State University for my junior year I felt that, one step at a time, I had finally arrived at my vocation. I was really fired up about teaching speech. In speech class, time and again, I'd see kids get up to talk in an agony of nervousness. I'd found that I, too, could panic. But I'd discovered ways to overcome my nervousness and I thought it would be great to pass these on. Sometime during everyone's life he's going to have to get an idea across to someone—a future boss, the PTA, a church group, a policeman. To help people handle these situations effectively became really meaningful to me. So I set my sights on that and put everything I had into it.

But new experiences and new opportunities can change our course, for it was in that year that I became Miss America.

My Miss America year certainly increased my confidence but it didn't take long to realize that this sense of confidence had to be tempered with humility if I was to be honest in my self-evaluation. It was easy to see that a person could be ruined by all this attention. Driving in splendid cars. The gift of an elegant wardrobe. The flowers, the crowds, people being so happy to see you. Realistically, I had to know that all this didn't go to Vonda Kay Van Dyke. It went to the image of Miss America.

To keep your perspective, whether you're a football hero or a homecoming queen or student-body president, you have to see clearly that the honors go with the position, and someone else will be stepping into it tomorrow—or next year. Youth is full of glowing moments, and we can afford to have our head in the clouds as long as we keep our feet on the ground. Certainly we will have worked for our moment of glory. Certainly we have to do our best to live up to the image. But as I traveled in this country, in Canada and Japan, and red carpets (sometimes green and purple ones) rolled out before me. I constantly reminded myself that all this appreciation belonged to the Miss America title. Not to me alone.

At the very beginning of my reign I prepared myself for the fact that it would end. I think the reason I got through the transition back to being a normal person without the possibility of becoming "a confused castoff thrown into a world without glamour and open hearts" was that I started it a year in advance.

For when the shining year ended I found that a lot of things beside the glamour and loving crowds had ended, too. I knew I would not become a speech teacher. Putting myself in the student's position, how would I feel if my teacher were a former Miss America? Whether they might look up to me, or thought I might look down on them, I just didn't see how we could ever have a normal student-teacher relationship. Nor did I feel I could return to my former campus. Here again the relationships wouldn't be relaxed and normal. Nothing, in fact, would ever be quite the same again.

I had the same sinking feeling everyone does when faced with losing the known and familiar—the safe enclosure of home, a familiar school, old friends. But I knew that negative feelings are a great enemy of progress. I would look on this as an opportunity to move forward into something new.

On the positive side I'd won enough scholarship money to complete my education at any campus I chose. I wasn't afraid of strange places or new things. So why not try a strange campus, and study something new? I had been intrigued with television when I'd done interviews, panel programs, and newscasts as Miss America. Both Northwestern and UCLA had good television departments and I applied and was accepted at both. I liked sunshine more than cold and snow so I enrolled in UCLA, and it was there I met a surgery resident, Andrew Laird.

By moving forward you can turn an ending into a beginning every time. Being Miss "A" moved me to UCLA where I got my B.A. in TV and my "Mrs." degree as well. I found both friendship and love were freely given to Vonda Kay and not an image.

But marriage and a college degree weren't an ending but a beginning, both of a new life and a new career. If we make the most of today and are open to tomorrow, we will find we are always beginning again.

How High Is Up?

If we want to find the answer to that question it's important for us to leave some room for God to make changes in our minds, hearts, and feelings. If we try to strap Him down with a statement we pledge ourselves to live with, we can limit our future and miss out on a big bundle of blessings. I've learned that it's necessary, in finding ourselves and our talents, to say a definite yes and a definite no in the now moment. It was a friend who gave me this valuable tip: "Never say never; never say always." True, we are caught in the rapids and whirl aimlessly if we worry about what we are *going* to do instead of dedicating ourselves to what we can do *now*. But we can wind up in that stagnant pond if we aren't open and flexible to the possibility of new and more wonderful things to come.

There is no conflict between staying flexible and setting goals. Each new opportunity, each new endeavor, each facet of talent we uncover demands that we choose exactly how far we will develop it.

A show magazine reporter recently asked me, "How far do you want to go with your singing career?"

I said simply, "I want to be good."

He sputtered. "You don't understand. Do you want TV? To branch into night clubs and acting? Or do you want to stay with the big conventions and fairs?"

I reminded him that he hadn't asked me *where* I wanted to go, but how *far*. Again I explained. "I want to be good. How far do I want to go? Until I'm best, I guess. That's my goal."

I really don't like to do things halfway. I've seen so many contestants in Miss America preliminaries who will not lose the extra five pounds they need to, or spend the few dollars on a good orchestration or costume, or work the extra hours on their talent act. When they turn up losers, they can soothe the sting with excuses of, "Well, if I had only done this or that I might have won." How do I know? You remember, it happened to me. No excuse is ever a soft pillow to fall back on. It's more like a needle that keeps pricking you. Now, to keep from falling into that trap, if I say yes to some activity, I give it all I've got.

If I try to be the best in everything that I do, to develop fully any abilities God gave me, and don't make my goal, at least I haven't failed Him or myself. When it's over, I can say I was honest with myself and just didn't do as well as I'd hoped. That's a lot more satisfying than continually wondering what would have happened *if* . . .

When I pursue a challenge I also select a goal. Singing, like everything else I do, is a challenge. When I come right out and tell a reporter that I want to be *best,* this would be a very high goal. Perhaps higher than I will ever come close to reaching. Realistically, I can only hope to be the best I can. The best within my capabilities. But I feel it is better to pick a high goal and never reach it than a series of minor goals that I can easily achieve.

I have found that if we stretch for the high goal, along the way our capabilities will grow and expand.

Then who knows what greater things the future will bring?

3

Out of Sight

On a flight between Chicago and Los Angeles I found myself sitting next to a very discouraged young lady. She was, she told me, returning from a visit to a girl friend who had been away at college for one semester.

"She's so changed I couldn't believe it," she said. "She's doing things my mom and dad told me not to do. She's gotten deeply involved in things I think are wrong. I'm concerned about her because she's my friend; but," she added honestly, "I'm more concerned about myself. I go away to school next year and I don't want that to happen to me."

This is a legitimate concern shared, one way or another, by all young people. On the one hand we look forward to being on our own, to achieving maximum independence and freedom. On the other we don't know quite what to expect nor how we'll handle it. We've seen some friend or campus success we've looked up to display great ability, set high goals, then get off course or flounder on his own.

We can prevent this, or correct our course, once we realize that, while choice is the rudder that guides our journey, character is the helmsman. Our own character dictates our choices.

What could I say to help the young lady on the plane and the rest of you faced with this dilemma? What had my own experience taught me?

Easy Does It

An old Chinese proverb says, "Patience is power; with time and patience the mulberry leaf becomes silk."

A friend of mine has a very precocious son. At sixteen he ran with an older crowd, had a B-plus average in high school, a good job, a car that was paid for. One thing he did not have was patience. At sixteen-plus-three-months he announced that he was ready to leave home and live in an apartment with some fellows. "Good," said his mother. "That's what we've been preparing you for, the day you'd be mature enough to live on your own." Since he was technically a minor she pointed out that his parents had a legal obligation to make sure he could handle it. "So," she said, "you can live at home for one week exactly as if you were in your own apartment, buy and cook your own food, take care of your clothes and laundry. If you check out, your dad and I will help you move."

The first and second days went well. The following afternoon, when he brought the fellows in for an impromptu snack, his mother's part of the refrigerator, which was off limits, was loaded with goodies. His own cupboard was bare. The next morning he ran out of toothpaste. His mother lent him some salt. He was late for school because he misplaced his car keys. By Friday night when he had a big date he didn't have a pair of clean socks or a fresh shirt. Very sheepishly he approached his mother. "Hey, mom," he said, "do you think I could move back home now?"

We all need the power of patience to ease ourselves gracefully into the adult world. Being on our own isn't accomplished by a single dramatic leap but by growing into it. By degrees we earn greater freedom and prove to *ourselves* that we can assume greater responsibility.

In my own case I lived at home through junior college. It was economically convenient. I thought I could make better grades, enter into more campus activities if I didn't have the additional struggle of adjusting to a whole new way of life. I didn't have the emotional need to prove anything. We were a very close family and I was an only child. My parents were strict but understanding and had given me increasing freedom as soon as I proved ready for it.

Looking back, I realize that this had another advantage. As I became an emancipated minor on my own at home I rediscovered my parents—as valuable friends. The affection remained the same but ties of dependence and authority gradually dissolved and were replaced by the mutual respect and ability to enjoy each other that we have today. If you go away to school in your freshman year you can still keep your folks in the picture by letter, by telephone, by weekends at home. An abrupt separation makes it difficult to establish a new relationship with them after you've begun your own way of life. At some point you have to start to relate as adult to adult if the new relationship is to be healthy and happy. If you sever all ties you stand to lose not only the wisdom they can share with you from their greater experience, but the natural growth into the new relationship.

When I was graduated from junior college a semester early, I decided that I'd use the extra semester for a fling at living away from home. Northern Arizona University was in the mountains a little over one-hundred-and-fifty miles from Phoenix, but once again I was moving by degrees. I could and did fly home many weekends.

The following year when I entered Arizona State, although it was less than twenty-five miles from home, I again lived on campus because my all-out effort in junior college made me eligible for the honor dorm. There we had few restrictions but our position of leadership imposed on all of us the obligation to live up to our "honor."

As Miss America I had unusual freedom in some respects but I was certainly not on my own. I had two chaperons who alternated monthly. Lucille Previti and Peggy O'Neil, both great gals, were with me for companionship and assistance in threading my way through a complicated schedule, not to impose restraint of conduct. If you won your way to that crown it was assumed you had developed the character to wear it with dignity. By the time I got to UCLA I was, as are most college seniors, zeroed in on getting my degree. This imposes the highest and safest form of restraint—self-discipline.

One definition of good character is "moral vigor or firmness especially as acquired through self-discipline." If we are impatient or dishonest with ourselves and move ahead of our ability to discipline ourselves, we can easily slip into doing things we know in our hearts are wrong. So self-discipline should be our ideal. Having the patience to develop it now can mean a less painful transition into responsible maturity.

Keep Involved

During my first experiment at living away from home I made a serious mistake. Because I had pushed myself so hard in junior college I decided to stay out of all activities at Northern Arizona. I was going to relax, go to a few classes and enjoy myself. I thought when I got away from home I'd have great freedom to do what I wanted to do and I'd need plenty of time in which to do it. This was all decidedly out of character for me and I paid for it.

I liked being on my own, but I found there really wasn't anything spectacular I wanted to do. Here I was in a small town with one theater and one bowling alley and all that time on my hands. I was very disillusioned. Not being involved, I found, creates a vacuum. And vacuums can be dangerous. They leave you wide open to all sorts of undesirable things. My own protection lay in the fact that I had already established pretty firm ideals. But this didn't keep me from gaining twenty pounds and being bored for the only time in my college career.

Live and Let Live

College affords you the opportunity to have a roommate. The first time you live with someone other than your family, especially if they are total strangers, is quite an experience. You really do have things to learn.

You learn some straight things about *you* because, while your family and friends are usually tolerant or at least polite about your shortcomings, if your peers are completely impersonal they can be very direct.

I had two roommates at Northern Arizona. I thought one of them was great and the other was hard to get along with. I ended up liking her very much, too, but we had to work at it.

She was, it turned out, meticulous—"a place for everything and everything in its place." I am definitely not meticulous. This is probably one of the worst things about me. Although I was aware of the shortcoming, no one before had ever pointed it out, stripped of either tolerance or concern. So there was tension. Finally I admitted my fault but explained that I wasn't accustomed to perfect order. I liked things clean, but perfect order seemed uncomfortably sterile. Since we were bound together for a semester we decided to live and let live. I'd be as tidy as I could be; she'd be as tolerant as she could be. The mutual effort didn't bring either of us to perfection, but we did learn to live together and like it.

Think for Yourself

To be truly independent means to be *self*-governing—not subject to the control of others. I've seen a lot of young people free themselves from the control of the older generation only to hand their lives over to the dictates of some group. Well, a group, whether it's a flock of sheep or one of the currently popular movements, follows a leader. That leader may be headed for Utopia or a precipice but the point is that if you are a follower, *you* are not headed for independence.

A safe rule is: *Work together. Think for yourself!*

When I lived in the honor dorm, four of us shared a suite. From the beginning we lived and worked together harmoniously and had a great time doing it. But you can't imagine four more different individuals.

We each had our own style of dressing, of doing our hair, our own way of doing our own thing. One of the girls was secretary to the college. Two were campus pompom girls. I was doing shows every day, a singing spot and ventriloquist act, in the Pepsi Cola Saloon at a fun park called Legend City, and getting ready to enter the Miss America Pageant *again*. My roommate was a brain, one of those rare individuals who could read an entire book at one sitting and almost quote it back to you. We were all very different and had different ideals and beliefs—and we were friends.

Find a Philosophy for Your Life

I feel that my philosophy, which is based on my faith in God, gives my life that extra, added something that is just *out of sight*.

A girl friend once said to me, "I don't have anything to believe in like you do." And I had to reply, "It's not that you don't have anything to believe in. It's that you have not chosen to believe in anything."

Our philosophy of life is what we choose to believe.

Without a lasting philosophy our character will be unstable, our conduct and relationships vacillating, our choices inconsistent. And we can flounder and flop no matter how great our ability or how high our goal.

There are a lot of philosophies today and I've talked to thoughtful young people all over the country and listened to what they have to say. I've heard them say, "My philosophy is to believe in the beautiful things of the world . . . beautiful people, the beauties of nature."

I agree that this is a good philosophy. It's great! But being a former Miss America I have to tell them that beauty passes. I have watched it fade, both in gardens and in people. So that's not a lasting philosophy.

I've heard them say, "I believe in a creed. I set myself a list of rules and live up to them. They are my guidelines, my creed of life."

Again, I can agree that this is a great philosophy. I do the same thing. I set rules and regulations and try to live by them. But I'm the first to admit that I'm not always successful. I break a lot of the rules I try to live up to. I just foul up and make mistakes. So that makes this philosophy not so lasting.

I've been told, "Well, I believe in my fellow man."

This is a prevalent philosophy and one that is important today. I believe in my fellow man and I'm thankful for people who do. But I'll also admit that even my best friends let me down sometimes. So that isn't lasting either.

I asked the discouraged young lady on the plane who was concerned about going away to school if she had a philosophy of life. She said, "Well, I guess so. I try to live by the rules my parents set for me. But," she added, "it isn't working very well because I'm beginning to think my parents don't know what they're talking about half the time."

This is not an abnormal reaction but it is disillusioning. It's helpful to remember that it may or may not be true. When Mark Twain was a boy of fourteen, it is said, he thought his father so ignorant that he couldn't bear to have him around. But when Mark Twain got to be twenty-one he was astonished at how much his father had learned in seven years. But let's face it. There are mature, wise parents. There are immature, unwise parents. There are actual problem parents. But wise, mature parents can't give us their wisdom or maturity any more than the others can prevent our growing up and finding our own. So I had to say to her, "Living by your parents' rules, whether they're right or wrong, isn't a lasting philosophy."

Then I told her what I've told the thousands of young people with whom I'm in contact. "I've found a philosophy that's lasting. Something I can believe in that I know is permanent. A philosophy of life based on faith in God. I like to term my philosophy as something firm I can stand on. I can really count on it no matter what is happening in the world around me. It's just secure, and a philosophy that's secure is very important to me. So I'd like to challenge you to look at different philosophies— and find the one that really works for you. I hope you find the one that has been satisfying to me."

"If you feel your philosophy and belief is the best one," asked a high-school girl hesitantly, "why aren't young people flocking to the churches?"

"Some of them are," I said, "because some of the churches are gearing themselves to young people—playing our kind of music, singing our kind of songs, expressing religion in a way we can understand. But I think you're confusing religion with faith. They're two completely different things. My philosophy is based on faith, not a religious creed or denomination."

My faith has some guidelines. They are found in what I stated in the Miss America pageant is the most important book I own. In it I found some really groovy thoughts—in other words, they're really packed with meaning for today.

If I should get depressed, I have to take on a positive attitude when I read: ". . . is your life full of difficulties and temptations? Then be happy, For when the way is rough your patience has a chance to grow. So let it grow, and don't try to squirm out of your problems. For when your patience is finally in full bloom, then you will be ready for anything, strong in character, full and complete" (James 1:2-4 LNT).

If I'm ever lonesome, it's a comfort to know that I have a friend in God who "sticketh closer than a brother" and never lets me down.

When I find myself going along with the crowd and not taking time to think for myself, I'm reminded in Romans 12:2: "Don't copy the fashions and customs of this world, but be a new and different person . . . in all you do and think" (LNT).

When I'm learning to live with others, I'm guided by some wise tips like these: "Work happily together. Don't try to act big. Don't try to get into the good graces of important people, but enjoy the company of ordinary folks. And don't think you know it all!" (Romans 12:16 LNT).

When I'm trying to keep my confidence in what I am now and what I should be, I think of 1 Timothy 4:12: "Don't let anyone think little of you because you are young. Be their ideal; let them follow the way you teach and live; be a pattern for them in your love, your faith, and your clean thoughts" (LNT).

These are just a few examples of why the Bible is my most important book. There is a lot of wisdom for today locked within these pages and with every new day I'm finding the Bible and my life of faith more exciting and more *out of sight* than ever.

4

What a Dummy Taught Me

Kurley Q was the only man who ever traveled with Miss America. He was red-headed, dimpled, impudent, wore a size four tuxedo, and I learned a lot from that young man.

Kurley came into my life when I was a sophomore in high school. Long before he was born in a cellar in Chicago I had been anticipating this blessed event.

One of my favorite television shows as a youngster was Paul Winchell and Jerry Mahoney. When my mother explained that the dummy wasn't really talking, that the man was making him talk, I tried to make a little voice of my own. I didn't do too well. So I decided I was just going to try to say letters without moving my lips. I practiced until I could manage almost every letter of the alphabet without any lip movement at all. Then I found that by placement of my voice I could make it deep, and by tensing my throat and pushing the sounds with my diaphram, out came this funny little voice. I began using it around the house to startle my friends and relatives. Quite on my own, and without even knowing the word, I had become a ventriloquist.

On my seventh birthday my parents gave me a simple dummy to go with the little voice and I persuaded my reluctant Sunday school teacher to let us sing a song and read a Bible story before the class. I had so much fun doing it and the kids enjoyed it so much that my mother helped me work up a little act. My dummy and I began to appear at birthday parties as well as other Sunday school classes. I had now become a performer and I found I really enjoyed entertaining people. Both of my first dummies were store-bought Jerry Mahoney dolls. My dream was to have my own dummy, designed for me alone. I was fifteen before I got him.

Enter Kurley Q

Frank Marshall was one of the finest creators of ventriloquist's figures in the United States. He was in Chicago, so to Chicago we went, my parents and I, and found our way to the cellar where he had his workshop. Mr. Marshall proved to be a very unusual man, quite old, with a chilly eye and a no-nonsense attitude. He let us know immediately that persuading him to create a dummy for me was not a matter to be undertaken lightly.

First he wished to know what I did with my dummy. I told him that I did Sunday school programs. "Do you get paid?" he demanded. "Well," I said, "sometimes." "I will not do a dummy for you," he said, "unless you get paid. It's not worth my while. I'm a professional and I do dummies for professional people." So I said, "Most of the time I do," without telling him that *if* I did it was rarely more than five or ten dollars.

Then he auditioned me. He looked at me, studied me, made me work with one of his figures. I hadn't expected this at all. Right then Kurley's life hung in the balance. It's odd to think that if I'd failed to pass Mr. Marshall's inspection I might never have known Kurley. Would my own life have been different? That I'll never know because abruptly Mr. Marshall said, "All right, I'll make you a dummy. Tell me what you want him to look like and I will determine from there." I said I wanted him to have a pug nose, dimples, blue grey eyes, and that I wanted to select his wig myself. He then took a picture of me, saying, "I want the dummy to go with you, to resemble you in some way," and we were dismissed.

Later when kids said, "Gee, you really look a little like your dummy," I always replied, "That's a compliment. That's the way it's supposed to be." It would not have been a compliment the day it arrived. While Kurley never became a raving beauty, the dummy in that box was the ugliest thing I'd ever seen. My parents and I were so disappointed. What I had asked for was there but it was so *bald*. Also it was a *thing*, an "it." Such a lifeless, inanimate *thing* that we couldn't think of a name.

"It" had arrived on Saturday and I had a Sunday performance scheduled in Flagstaff so we rushed off to the doll hospital in Phoenix and I bought it a very curly auburn red wig. Then we sat around trying to think of a catchy name that would go with Vonda, or Kay, or even Van Dyke. My father suggested Vernon, but it didn't look like Vernon to me. The best I could think of was Epod, which was Dope spelled backward. On Sunday morning we hastily decided on Kurley because of the wig, with a K, because of Vonda Kay, and off we went to Flagstaff.

Kurley and I had had very little time to get acquainted. All of the fingering and technical things on the inside were completely different from anything I'd used before. Right in the middle of our program I lost the string. Kurley couldn't open his mouth. There I was in front of an entire church congregation and Sunday school with a dummy that couldn't talk. I didn't know what to do so I looked at him and said, "What's the matter?" He just turned his head to me. I said, "How come you're not talking?" I leaned my ear over his mouth, listened and said, "Couldn't you have done that before we came up here?" The audience immediately understood that he needed to excuse himself so, amid great laughter, we stepped out of sight, I found the string, brought him back, and we went on with the program. Later we met informally with the kids. They asked Kurley questions and really got involved. When I got up to leave, one of the little girls said, "Goodbye, Kurley Q."

The dummy had come to life. Kurley had gotten himself a last name, begun to develop his own distinct personality, and taught me my first lesson.

The Value of Laughter

From our very first performance Kurley insisted that I learn the value of laughter—whether to get out of an embarrassing situation, to make a point, to break tension—and particularly the value of laughing at myself. Kurley was a master at putting me down.

Since this was the way his personality developed I had no choice but to go along with him. Sometimes it was totally impromptu, as it had been in the church. Sometimes it was carefully calculated, as in our Miss America talent competition which was limited to exactly three minutes. For this performance I collected card files of new jokes, tried them out at Legend City, had reactions timed with a stop watch, tabulated results in an enlarging notebook, until I had statistics on surefire laughs tested on at least five audiences.

The point I had to make in those three minutes was *Arizona*. Experience at America's Junior Miss Pageant had taught me that the judges don't have time to remember your name. I had to brand myself "Miss Arizona." A western joke just didn't make it; we'd tried hundreds. Then one day, while at a luncheon with Barry Goldwater, the emcee introduced us as the future Mr. President and the future Miss America. Would I dare to dabble in politics? Maybe I wouldn't, but Kurley would. And Kurley fancied puns. So to open the talent competition I asked him, "Kurley, have you noticed all the beautiful blue water here in Atlantic City?" Kurley replied, "That's nothin'. In *Arizona* we've got Goldwater."

At Legend City I'd learned from Kurley the psychological value of having most of the laughter at my own expense. Letting the dummy put me down hinted at humility, subconsciously shifting the audience to my side. My responses were designed to show patience, tolerance, the ability to rise above any situation. Kurley was beautifully impudent at Atlantic City. Our dialogue went like this:

VONDA Notice all those lights on the stage?
KURLEY Yeah, and they hurt my eyes.
VONDA You don't have to look at the lights. You can look at me.
KURLEY That hurts worse.
VONDA Are you insinuating that I'm ugly?
KURLEY Well?
VONDA I expect an apology.
KURLEY Okay. I'm sorry you're ugly.

Fortunately the judges didn't agree with him, but Kurley went right on putting me down from the beginning to the end of my reign and everybody found him delightful. He had a way of opening our performances by singing, "There she is, Miss America. There she is, big deal!" before I could shut him up. I'll admit he was naughty, but the laughter broke the ice.

On the night before my reign ended I was on my own. Kurley was back in our hotel room. But by this time he had me trained. We were rehearsing for the final night of the Pageant when I would hand over my crown. I was practicing my final march and Bert Parks was singing, "There she is, Miss America . . ." when I suddenly realized how uptight all the contestants were. I remembered my own feelings one year before and said, "Excuse me, Bert, but I'd like to sing my own song." Taking my cue from Kurley I improvised, "Here I am, Miss America. Here I am, big deal. With so many beauties, I took the world by storm, with my all-American big fat form. There she is, blowing hot air she is—I'm Miss America!"

The whole place broke up and the laughter really eased the tension for those girls.

Kurley didn't mellow with age. On the contrary, he got naughtier. As we worked together more and more he became so much his own personality that I honestly felt sometimes he said things I hadn't thought of.

One such occasion was just after my first album for Word Records was released when Kurley and I did a fund-raising banquet for a charity organization. The emcee turned out to be the disc jockey for a local religious station which, I'd been told, had *banned* the record because it was too groovy. I just couldn't believe a station would turn their back on a record that said all the right things even if it did swing a little. But the disc jockey said it was true; they couldn't even use it to advertise my coming. I thought this was ridiculous but there was nothing I could say.

This didn't hold true for Kurley. The minute we stood up he initiated a dialogue by saying the man didn't like me. I said, "Of course he likes me." "Well," said Kurley, "I don't like him. I don't like him because he doesn't like you." "But," I defended, "We've just had a delightful conversation." "Take my word for it," Kurley insisted, "he doesn't like you." "What in the world is wrong with you?" I asked. "Your record is banned on his station, that's how I know." The audience went up in a roar. Up to then I was definitely in control, but at this point Kurley got carried away. Just as the laughter died he popped off, "That's all right folks. Right after the program you can step right up and buy your own dirty record." This time I really did shut him up. Of course it brought another roar but the amusing thing was that within ten minutes all the records were sold out. Kurley even seemed to know the commercial value of laughter.

The Value of Money

When you're a toddler there's absolutely no difference between a coin and a button. They're both just something you mustn't put in your mouth. Later on a coin becomes a fun thing you can throw at a plate for a baby duck, although it's hard to see why it wouldn't be just as good a trick with a button. Then one bright day you discover that you can exchange a coin for a candy bar. Money is valuable. It will buy *things*. Squirt guns. Peanuts. *Cars*. And the initiative to earn is born.

My parents were wise to try to guide my spending in my earliest years. I was eight years old when we went to the bank and opened my first savings account. I was proud of this and managed to save much more than I spent. That lesson in saving is one I have always been grateful for.

In high school I learned that, if you're willing to *work,* a talent that has become a hobby can be transformed into a profession. You can make it earn for you and still have fun. Kurley was a professional dummy. Mr. Marshall had made that clear. When Kurley came into my life I had a new goal. We had a ladder to climb together. As we improved our act we began getting as much as $35 for some of our appearances at high school proms and big Sunday school rallies. The rewards were sweet. When I fell in love with a fluffy pink evening dress my family considered too expensive, I could buy it myself.

By the time I was a senior in high school I'd learned something else. Just wanting money for the things it would buy was an adolescent value, useful to get you started, but a trap if you didn't go beyond it. The real value of money was the adult freedom it gave you to make your own choices.

My parents had always said they were going to send me through college. Without asking them I thought the deal would be that if they paid my way I would go to the college of their choice. I thought then this was only fair. I think so still. The idea that a young adult could do what he wanted to do (or buy what he wanted to buy) with Daddy's bank account I just couldn't see. I attended Phoenix Christian High School. I got a fine education, had a ball, made wonderful friends. But as a young adult I wanted to go to a secular college and see what it was like in the big, wide wonderful world. Thus I felt I had to pay for my own education. To win enough money in scholarships, to earn enough money to give me that right to independence became a much more important goal than being able to buy *things.*

Kurley helped me all the way.

In the end I think Frank Marshall would have considered being midwife at Kurley's birth well worth his while. Miss Arizona gave me a $1,000 scholarship, Miss Congeniality another $1,000, and the Miss America crown brought a $10,000 scholarship. During my Miss America year, partly because of Kurley, I had more bookings than any previous queen. While it's hard to set up a trampoline, or do an impromptu dance or dramatic reading, Kurley fitted in everywhere. He traveled and lived quietly in his small suitcase, to emerge always fresh, smiling, and ready to go to work. Beyond his rather extensive wardrobe he had no physical requirements. He was a good trouper and together we made it—all the way to the top.

Exit Kurley Q

My theme song with Kurley, the one we sang at the Pageant, was, *Whatever we do, wherever we go, we're gonna go through it together.*

I think, at the time, I really believed it.

From the day he arrived, hairless and nameless, until the end of my reign as Miss America, Kurley and I had been separated only once. That semester when I went to Northern Arizona University I left Kurley at home because he had a way of getting me involved whether I liked it or not. But I was quite sad without him. I even dreamed about him once. For most girl children there is one doll that becomes utterly real—a playmate, a friend, a living entity to talk to and fuss over. I had had one, when I was very young, named Sally. Like her, Kurley had become real to me. During the time we worked together at Legend City I talked to him more than I did to any living person. He was part of my life.

But the last and most valuable lesson I learned from Kurley Q was to say good-bye to yesterday to make way for tomorrow.

Today Kurley is in retirement, sitting quietly at home in his little suitcase. Occasionally I bring him out to sit in the room, or we do a performance together for a benefit for young children for old times sake. But professionally I am on my own at last.

You see, Kurley and I reached our joint goal during my Miss America year. After that the challenge was gone. I had been a ventriloquist since I was six years old. I was good, the *best* within my capabilities. But I was finding ventriloquism a limited field. There wasn't much demand for Kurley and me at a really high professional level. Also, more and more I found I could convey things through a song that just wouldn't fit into dialogue. Kurley would never let me be serious and, while we both knew the value of laughter, when I wanted to say something from my heart I always had to do it alone.

I could give more of myself in a singing performance than I could when there were two personalities in a ventriloquist act. I could become a more integrated person. And as a singer I couldn't be my best with Kurley helping me all the time. I realized that the first time I walked out on a stage alone and forgot the words to my song. If Kurley had been there I could have said, "Why did you forget the words? You really are a dummy!" This time I had to play it straight, get out of it myself, and make sure it didn't happen again. If I was ever to perfect my technique as a singer I had to let Kurley go.

Part of the pain of growing up is to lose the world of make-believe, to realize that your doll is only a doll, that your toy plane will never get off the ground. But only as we say good-bye to the doll or the plane that meant so much to us yesterday do we make way for the living child or a trip to the moon tomorrow. We can always keep some of the magic of make-believe if we realize that it was our wonderful power of imagination that gave life to the doll or the plane or to Santa Claus—or to Kurley Q. And that we never lose.

When I stepped up to a new life after my reign, the new challenge was to transform *Miss America: Talent—Ventriloquism,* into *Vonda Kay Van Dyke: Career—Singer.*

My dummy was part of the old life. As I said "Good-bye, Miss America" I was also going to be gradually saying "Good-bye, Kurley Q."

Sometimes I miss him. But he is still a good trouper. When I take him out of his little suitcase he is always smiling.

5

The Secrets of Success

When I first began pageant competition I naturally studied the big winners. They came in various shapes, colors, and sizes, but they all had one thing in common. I noticed it first when I was runner-up in the Miss Phoenix pageant. The girl who won was somehow above us all from the beginning. She was beautiful, yes, but she was something else! In our minds she was the winner even before the judges picked her. The next girl who won over me also had something about her that spelled winner. There was an aura about them that I couldn't label at the time, but I can now.

Today, recording artists that I most admire are Barbra Streisand for her ability, Vicki Carr for her feeling for a song, and Lana Cantrell for her voice quality. Although I have never seen these girls in live performances, on stage I have enjoyed and admired most Lisa Minelli for her sheer drive and Anita Bryant for her dramatic interpretation of lyrics. Different, as they are, each of these highly successful young ladies has that same aura. Each seems to be saying, "I'm me—and glad of it."

The aura of success is self-confidence.

I've worked with many outstanding evangelists across the country. One of the interesting and really challenging speakers is Bill Glass, great defensive end for the Cleveland Browns. He's a huge guy with a forceful delivery who's still capable of being simple. Working in his Crusades I've found that when he talks about his faith in Christ it has a tremendous impact on both young and old. He gave those audiences his formula for success: "Confidence, courage, causes." *Confidence* from within, *courage* to get out and try and do, and *causes* to provide the objective.

Self-confidence, as Bill emphasized, is vital. Whether our objective is to win a contest, or to succeed as a person on the wider horizons of life, or to witness for Christ, we have to start by believing we can do it.

Color Me Unique

It's amazing that so many people, young and old, not only fail to realize that they lack confidence in themselves, but how dangerous that lack can be. Self-confidence that is genuine and abiding, deep and sustaining is a scarce personal quality. It seems that the bully and the egotist, the dictator and the show-off are types that do not really have belief in themselves.

If we look, it becomes fairly obvious that antisocial or weak behavior stems from insecurity. But what of the rest of us? Do we realize that, if we fail to develop confidence when we're young, we could become phony people for life? We'd go to a certain church or pick a certain denomination because "religious social cats" attend there. We'd dress ourselves trying to match perfectly the covers of the fashion magazines, whether the styles looked well on us or not. We girls would search the beauty columns and squander our money trying to look like something we're not, while the fellows study their favorite athletes and try to appear like someone they're not either. Or we'd all copy the mannerisms of people we admire. We'd soon find ourselves a bland montage of black and white photostats of the things and people around us, lacking all the color and originality and glamour that could be ours.

The only thing that can add hues to our outside is to bring out the glowing hues from inside, the deep down part that's really us. The part of us that unashamedly splashes bright tones of "I'm me" all over us and the people we meet. It's the deep blues of sadness and sincerity; the rich reds of compassion and love; the yellow of sunny smiles and deep happiness. These are the only basic colors, but from them we can mix every tint and shade.

So with these basic ingredients of personality, working with exactly what we have—making the most of them physically, mentally, and spiritually—we can create someone very special. That special someone will be the unique and original *you.*

If we're not satisfied with ourselves as we are, or with the way we look (and no one, I've found, is ever completely satisfied), the answer is not to try to become like someone else. Obviously, we need all the help we can get. And equally obviously, as soon as we can hear or read, all manner of help is available to us. We can and should know what the principles of good health or a sound education can do for us. We can and should look around us, observe and admire the best qualities in others, listen to and study the innumerable suggestions that the media and the advertiser are sending our way for improving both the male and female of the species. The question is, How do we digest this abundance of riches and still keep from becoming just a photocopy of a hundred other people? And the answer I've found is, *Adapt, don't imitate.*

Take a look at your own strengths and weaknesses and when a suggestion or quality appeals to you ask yourself: Is it right for me? If so, what part is applicable to my personal needs? Will it emphasize my strengths or strengthen my weaknesses? Do I completely agree with what is to be accomplished?

Be creative and imaginative when you apply new knowledge to your face, your personality, or your life. This is how the original full-color portrait comes into being.

It takes time for the potential masterpiece to take shape. You'll experiment, work, fail, succeed, fail, and try again, as I've discovered. But the rewards of becoming that unique person are worth the time and effort. The real self is the only self we can believe in. The goal of self-discovery and self-improvement is self-confidence, the first requisite for success.

The Three Ps

As Bill Glass has his personal three-C formula for success, so I have a three-P formula for making the most of ourselves. Each is a step that builds confidence, gives us something firm to stand on as we climb toward our goal. They are: *plan, prepare, pray.*

While I firmly believe with the poet that "a man's reach should exceed his grasp," I just as firmly believe we need a practical procedure telling us where to put our feet. When we have an end in view, we need to grasp all of the details, do our homework of *planning, prepare* in every way we can, *pray* for the extra help we need, and reach with all our might.

It has been said that men don't plan to fail—they just fail to plan. So many of us are running around *doing* that we don't have much time for *thinking.* We let our lives get complicated and involved, or we are so dependent on people that we rarely take time off to evaluate, to plan. Life, if you're going to be successful at it, means time away from crowds and rushing. Planning involves much thought, and for thought you need time. I have learned to take time to be alone—and I've learned to like it. That precious time can lead to a successful evening meal, expenditures to match your income or allowance, meeting your daily schedule with minutes to spare, or taking your personal inventory and working out plans to make the most of yourself.

If it hadn't been for the encouragement of Mrs. Leo Ryan, a lovely lady who had been a judge in one of the Miss Phoenix pageants, I might not have gone back for that third try for the Miss America title. As they sometimes say, though, "Three is a charm." I won my first title, Miss Tempe, with no difficulty. I was the only contestant who showed up. This is not confidence-making. Twice I had been a runner-up, and that doesn't do much for your ego either. Now I faced the county competition and, if I won that, in a short month and a half, Miss Arizona. What could I do to prepare myself to the best of my ability? I had once been told, "To handle yourself, use your head—to handle others, use your heart." Since I had only myself to work with, I'd have to begin by using my head. So I sat down alone with pencil and paper to weigh my strengths and weaknesses and plan my action.

To really evaluate ourselves it's important to scrape away all the debris, get rid of preconceived ideas of what we are like, or what other people have told us we are like—good or bad. We need to throw all negatives out of our minds. This doesn't mean we are going to lie to ourselves. It means we're not going to wear shades but take a clear-eyed look at what we find to work with. It's equally important to forget that girl on the magazine cover. Her image can blur our vision, discourage us, or tempt us into imitating instead of adapting our knowledge.

Golf champion Sam Snead once gave golfers the perfect advice for any contestant who worries about the competition. "Forget your opponents," he said, "always play against par." In working with yourself, par is the best "you" that you can be. You are competing against your own best. So we're going to take a positive attitude toward everything we find—and make the best of it. If we have strengths, can we make them stronger? Emphasize them? If we have weaknesses, can we correct them? If we can't correct, can we minimize them?

I had two obvious weaknesses. My walk was a little clumsy. Practice could help correct this. And I was a good five pounds overweight. This, too, I could correct. I knew the rules of diet. All I had to do was adapt them. Good-bye hot fudge sundaes and chocolate cake.

The two aspects of the Miss America competition where you can show the most individuality are talent and the extemporaneous answer to a question at the end of each contest. Kurley Q was definitely a strength. In fact so many of our friends and relatives considered him a unique and interesting talent that they talked me into my first contest and this last one. But good as our fans thought we were, we knew we could and must be better. I was carrying a full load at Arizona State, but by budgeting my time and working a little harder at Legend City, we could improve. But, oh, those extemporaneous questions! I could speak well, but my answers lacked that instant concise strength and meaning they needed. I was not a genius, and I couldn't see any way to become one overnight. So the only solution in sight was to say a little prayer for the extra help I needed and think carefully before I opened my mouth.

My plans had swung into the preparation stage when I discovered a legitimate handicap. As a child I'd been hit by a car that resulted in a broken leg. After weeks in the hospital in traction, at home in a cast, at school on crutches, it had healed completely. But as I stood before the mirror practicing my pageant stance, I noticed that the leg which had been injured was slightly smaller than the other, one fourth of an inch at the calf by actual measurement. Instead of hitting the panic button, smothering myself with negatives and self-pity, I sat down quietly to think. I had heard of athletes who had overcome far greater handicaps and developed not only physical but mental and spiritual muscles in the overcoming.

What could I *do?* I hadn't time before the county or Miss Arizona pageants to correct this—if such a thing was possible. So I'd minimize. In my store of knowledge was the fact that dark colors tend to minimize and lighter ones add. I'd adapt this to my situation. For street wear I'd wear a slightly darker nylon on the larger leg. It helped. But for swimsuit? I began practicing my modeling position reversing my forward leg. This way the problem would always be in the background. It was unnatural at first, but eventually I managed it. Along with this, since I now felt shaky in the swimsuit competition, I felt I needed a change of attitude. I remembered a girl I'd seen at a pageant long ago who walked with a funny, carefree little bounce. True, every time she walked out everyone laughed. I didn't want that. But she had that air—happy, full of life and fun, like she was on vacation having a great time and about to jump into the ocean. A smooth glide for evening gowns, yes, but, I thought, that's the air you should have in a swimsuit. Could I adapt it to me? I developed a little spring between my steps, so slight you hardly noticed it, but it gave that air. Then I decided, after much hesitation, to put aside my customary dark suit and wear a gold one that sparkled under the lights. It simply shouted confidence. It stated so positively, "Here's one gal who's not afraid to walk out in a swimsuit!" that I hoped no one would notice my knees were shaking. When I later won the swimsuit competition in the state pageant, I realized my efforts were worth it.

And when it came time for the extemporaneous answer, well, I said another little prayer and waited. The question was on the nuclear test-ban treaty. I could feel my family tensing because they knew I didn't have time to keep up with current events in any depth. But I answered brilliantly, adding specific facts and figures! During the applause that followed I breathed a sigh of relief and later shared my secret with my astounded parents. While having the car washed that afternoon I had read one article in a news magazine on—that's right—the nuclear test-ban treaty. It looked like it was my prayer that worked most on that question.

Private prayer, to me, is a very personal thing—the way one individual talks directly to God. I know there are many people with no significant religious belief who think being a Christian is copping-out, putting your problems on Somebody else. I don't feel that way because I still have the problems. They're just easier to live with. I really have confidence that I've got Somebody who can help me. I can say, "Look, I've got a problem that I don't know how to solve. Help me find the solution." I don't believe God is going to do *for* me what He can only do *through* me. I'm certainly not asking for miracles; if I get the guidance, I expect to do the work. So after the county pageant I prayed again.

I didn't get an "answer from God." I got an idea. It came while I was in the university library looking up something in a book of quotations. Running down the index, I thought, wow, a lot of these are the subjects usually brought up at the pageants —beauty, character, citizenship, education, honesty, humility, success, values—and what the greatest minds of all times said about them. I could "prepare" by making a list of general topics, writing down two or three short, concise quotes, and memorizing them. Once I'd thoroughly committed them to memory I had to practice rephrasing them, or adapting them, to wrap up my answers to specific questions. So, with my roommates and with my family at home, I began playing "Ask me a question." I was tickled to see their heads turn in amazement as I'd briefly give my thoughts and climax them with what "someone" once said.

This really helped build my confidence. If I couldn't think under pressure. I could always turn to the thoughts of someone wiser. Even if my own thoughts came clearly, the quotes gave me a tag line that had real impact.

In the winner's circle, when I was wearing the Miss Arizona crown, there were cameras, crowds of people, comments, and questions. One newsman remarked on my concise and meaningful answers to the extemporaneous questions: "The touch of the quote and all." I simply smiled and said, "Thank you, sir." This was my secret, one I've never shared before.

During the nine months of my reign as Miss Arizona I continued to plan and prepare to represent my state and myself to the best of my ability. I worked on my wardrobe, my make-up, my hair-dos. Kurley and I polished and re-polished our performance. Part of my winnings was a scholarship to a health studio. There I did double sets of exercises on one leg, and by the time I went to Atlantic City, measurements showed this had been corrected. I also worked on my quotations, picking more words, memorizing more selections, so I'd have a broader choice of reference. I felt that even if I didn't use them I would have the confidence that I could handle anything.

At the Atlantic City pageant my questions were so personal—about the Bible and my religion—that I couldn't take the answers from any outside source. But during the Miss America year I automatically made frequent references to those quotes. If they would fit in with what I was saying, I'd suddenly remember them. Since then, in speaking and in writing, I've found such sources invaluable. I've discovered there are many fine collections. Reading these books appeals to me not only because I enjoy them, but because I'm learning something at the same time.

The reason I've decided to share my secret now is that I've come to believe, even if you're not in the public eye, it stimulates growth and adds rich colors to the mind to assimilate inspiring words by people who knew what they were talking about and said it the way we would like to say it.

If we haven't the time or capacity to read widely here is capsuled wisdom we can apply to everyday life. As Sir Winston Churchill said, "The quotations when engraved on the memory give good thoughts." And good thoughts not only give confidence but an excellent springboard for planning, preparing, praying.

6

The Weeping Winner

One of the quotes engraved on my memory is, "The cheerful loser is the winner." I had reason to know this is so. Because I had tried to smile from the inside each time I lost, and because I had been discouraged without giving up, had done my best and had tried my hardest, I finally won the right to represent my state at Atlantic City.

But I had no capsuled wisdom to explain a "tearful winner"— and that's what I turned out to be. The first time I reached a goal I really thought was impossible, what turned on was a flood of genuine tears.

Because I understand it now, because I did gain wisdom from the experience, I'd like to tell it as it was.

When the countdown started on that huge, hushed stage and I found myself in the top ten, then in the top five, instead of smiling I became very serious. Finally there were two girls left, Karen Carlson, Miss Arkansas, and Vonda Kay Van Dyke, Miss Arizona, seated side by side. Then I did smile because I knew Karen was going to win. She was a wonderful girl, and I was truly happy for her. When they announced Karen as first runner-up, and I finally believed what I heard, I began to cry. I looked at Karen as if to say, "I'm glad I'm me, but I wish you were Miss America."

All the other girls walked down the runway with beautiful,

brave smiles, and there I was, wearing the crown—with nothing but tears. I was unique all right. Color me sad!

I was totally surprised, which could account for a nervous reaction, but the amazing thing was that, deep down, I suddenly didn't know if I wanted to win. They say that in moments of stress sometimes your whole past flashes before your eyes. With me it was my whole future. I thought, Oh, my goodness! I have all my plans made for next year. My college courses set, a great girl I want to room with, reservations in the new dorm, my job at Legend City waiting for me. Suddenly all these plans were up in the air. I was going to have to be away from home for a whole year, and not go back even if I wanted to.

I was trying to clear my head. I told myself, You must say all the right things. Now that you're Miss America it's more important than ever to say the right things.

But what were those right things? I felt a great weight of responsibility, like I was dissolving into the runway. I was getting into something that I really know little about. I'd read all the literature that came; I'd signed the contracts—every girl does before she goes to Atlantic City. But I couldn't remember the details. I thought, What does the contract say? What am I going to have to do?

I didn't know and I was afraid.

I slept little that night. I had made a discovery, one I think too few young people are made aware of. Success has a price. I hadn't come really prepared to pay it.

The next morning I had my first press conference. All the careful coaching my good friend Sandy Gibbons had prepared me with—"All right, I'm a reporter, you're Miss Arizona, here are my questions"—got washed away in another flood of tears I couldn't control.

At the luncheon for all the contestants, their parents, and sponsors—everyone who had any connection with the pageant—I had regained my composure—temporarily. But when I got up to speak I felt such a closeness, such a real affection for them all, that my prepared speech went right out of my head. I spoke from my heart, improvising on Kurley's and my song. "I just want you to know that you've given me the greatest award I could have—Miss Congeniality. I will be representing you, and whether I'm qualified or not, I don't know. Just remember that, because you're my friends, wherever I go, whatever I do, you'll have had a hand in it."

Before I got half-way through, everyone in the room, including me, was crying. Men were pulling out handkerchiefs, all the girls were in tears, there wasn't a dry eye in the house. The following year when Debbie Bryant, the new Miss America, so beautiful, so poised, got up and gave a lovely speech everybody applauded. I couldn't help thinking to myself, this year everybody is so happy. Last year they wept.

Just the other day a neighbor of mine told a friend that she lived next to a Miss America, and she identified me. The friend, recalling my soggy coronation, said, "Oh, she's the human one!" I'd like to accept that explanation but the truth I want to share with you is that, because I had not prepared to *win,* my self-confidence was swept away not by a wave of humility, but of self-doubt. With all my planning and preparations I was only climbing a ladder, accepting a challenge, having fun doing it. I had prepared to *lose,* cheerfully.

I think that all too often, to protect ourselves, or because we think it shows humility, we young people unconsciously limit our reach by accepting the *probability* of failure. The *possibility* is always there. For that, everyone keeps telling us, we *must* prepare. But if we accept the *probability,* success can take us by surprise and knock us off balance.

I could rationalize it because I had lost before, because I had been ignored all during my week in Altantic City (I was the only contestant who never got her picture in the paper), because I had won Miss Congeniality (and no girl who had ever gotten that recognition from the other contestants had ever gotten top spot from the judges). I was holding a negative picture. But rationalization doesn't help when you're faced with reality.

Here I was, Miss America, and to date I hadn't made a great success of winning.

My own first aid in all such situations was at hand. I prayed. I don't remember now what words I used, or if I used any. Duke Ellington, whose sacred music is being played today in Christian churches and Jewish synagogues, says, "Every man prays in his own language, God understands them all." Maybe my tears were my prayer. But somehow I got through the first day. The second day after the pageant Dr. Billy Graham visited me and my parents and we all knelt down and asked God's guidance for me during the coming year. Later, in talking with him, I got a clear picture not only of what the Miss America image meant to young people, but of what might be my unique contribution to that already colorful image.

I had a cause—my faith and belief in Jesus Christ. If I could quietly inspire one young person to find a new life—a truly exciting and abundant life—in Christ, then to me my reign would be a success. With His help I could live every day with courage and confidence. I began to look forward to the year away from home, to the new places and people and opportunities, with a positive sense that it could be one of the happiest, smilingest years of my life. And of course, it was.

The Fourth P

The wisdom I gained from being a weeping winner has caused me to add a fourth P to my original formula. I call it the *positive picture*. To me it means that, no matter how high we are reaching, no matter how far our goal seems to exceed our grasp, we need to mentally picture ourselves as having achieved it.

I've found this technique really works wonders in little as well as big things.

When I say wonders, I really mean it. The first time I unconsciously used it and saw the results, I was so startled I couldn't accept it. I was away at college and my Uncle John was coming to visit. Since we had a limited choice between the bowling alley and an old movie, I decided he should take me bowling. I hadn't bowled in years but my score was astonishing. The only explanation I could imagine was that I'd been mentally bowling strikes for two weeks before he arrived and that the mental practice had been translated into action. But that seemed nonsense. Today I know it isn't. Having used the technique consciously I find it makes very good sense.

Within the last few years I've acquired golf clubs and taken lessons from a first-rate professional. This game has to be one of the greatest challenges ever and I'm still not good, but I've found that if I take even as little as five or ten minutes prior to my lesson to concentrate, to mentally picture myself doing perfectly what I had been taught, I could succeed in putting into practice almost all the principles my pro has been drilling me on in our previous lesson. I can save time and money and build my confidence by just being mentally prepared and ready to move on to something new.

When I first began singing I wasn't really sure exactly what I wanted to sound like. Then as the weeks and months progressed I began to form a *mental image* of precisely how I hoped to sound. Before a show or a program I mentally go through each song and the way I'll be singing it. By hearing my songs and my thoughts, I know before I walk on stage just how they will come out when I get in front of the people who are there to listen. If I'm with people I limit myself to just the mental run-through, but I've found concentration on that mental picture of what I am going to do essential. Now all that remains is to keep at it until my voice matches that picture.

That may be an endless project. I may be reaching for the unreachable star. But I know that if I stick with the four Ps at least I can close the gap. And so can you!

7

The Magnetic Personality

The love of popularity has been defined as "the love of being loved." And that—for every man, woman, and child—is the name of the game. So let's admit it. We all want to be loved.

No success is truly successful, no happiness is truly happy, unless we feel that someone cares. As has been said, "Happiness held is the seed; happiness shared is the flower." Without someone to share our struggles and victories we are incomplete, isolated, alone. Adults try to fill this void with the substitutes of status, wealth, power, but young people are wide open, particularly vulnerable to this sense of not belonging.

So perhaps the most important secret of successful living is how to develop a personality so magnetic that it will not only make us popular with our peers and the opposite sex today, but attract all kinds of people to us today and tomorrow. Once we have self-confidence, the next area in which we need confidence is in our relationship with others.

How do we develop it?

Our generation is deluged with suggestions that amount almost to mass hypnosis assuring us that our popularity depends on how we look on the outside. The emphasis is placed on what I call "packaging." If we anoint ourselves in the prescribed fashion, if we decorate our exteriors with enough buttons and bows and paint and glitter, we have it made. But have we?

I am reminded of the hours I used to spend as a kid making mud pies. Sometimes masterpieces would be slipped on the dinner table. They were beautiful and invitingly delicious, the outside decorated carefully with everything from seeds to jelly beans and marbles. They were very attractive pies—until you looked under the surface.

Isn't this like some people? Fixing up the outside may get you a first look, even a second. But it won't satisfy anyone looking for a deeper relationship. We can smell like a rose, be clothed like a lily, and still be a wallflower.

I had a sad little note recently from a gal who said, "I don't have any friends cause my nose is turned up and my face is bumped out." I want to assure her, and reassure you, that if you're lacking in friendships it is definitely not as a result of any of your physical features or defects. Remember, what colors an attractive outside personality are the glowing hues we bring up from deep down inside.

There are young people today so convinced of this that they have gone to the opposite extreme. They put the mud on the outside. If they're beautiful people on the inside then others should sense it, mud and all, and be willing to dig for the pearls.

Once again, I'm for the middle ground. Let's admit that the way we look determines that first impression and that it is important (and fun) to package ourselves as appealingly as we can. It gives us an initial confidence, for example, to watch our diet and skin care if we're "bumped out"; to take the curlers out of our hair before we go to the market; to be neat and clean. But if you're feeling insecure, nervous, and sorry for yourself on the inside, if you're radiating the sulks or dissatisfaction, it will do more to demagnetize your personal attraction than a pimple on your forehead. I've never cared particularly for my nose, either. In fact I wanted mine pug. And occasionally I have skin problems. Don't we all? But people don't seem to notice if I have a friendly manner and a bright smile going for me, 'cause then they start looking deeper than my surface wrappings.

And when they look deeper, what will they find?

The answer to that question will determine whether we become friends, nod as acquaintances, or pass by as strangers. My shiny smile may dazzle someone for a moment, but the magnet that draws them into a deeper relationship will be what they find in my heart.

Learning to Care

It was in the entertainment world that I found the key to overcoming nervousness and relating to others on a new and deeper level.

After my Miss America year I was very sure of myself and my ability to relate. I even had a few tips to pass on to those who still suffered insecurity and self-consciousness, things I'd discovered in speech classes, tricks I'd picked up in pageant competition. A former Miss America had suggested that, in order to keep a natural, alert smile, you should recite the alphabet to keep your mind busy. I preferred to carry on an imaginary conversation with the crowd. I'd spot an unsmiling face and say mentally, "Oh, so you don't like me. Well, I like you anyway." In speech class they'd suggested that, to ease stage-fright, you look over people's heads or at the clock at the back of the hall. This seemed to me noticeable and wrong. People know when you're looking at them and they appreciate it. But sometimes it's hard to look them in the eye and smile. A fellow contestant once shared her secret for an instant smile. She said, "Just look into the audience and imagine that every man you see is sitting there in red underwear. If that doesn't make you smile, nothing will."

So for years I'd been saying confidently, "No, I never get nervous in front of people—whether one or one thousand." But the day my entertainment career actually began I found myself nervous, insecure, without a trick up my sleeve.

My husband, Andy, had left for a year's tour of duty with the First Marine division in Vietnam. I had finally, by degrees, arrived at being totally on my own, taking care of my own bills, keeping my own apartment, being my own boss. My hours were my own. I really had no one at all to talk with about what I was going to do that day. There were no restrictions—and no directions. It was a funny, empty feeling. I was faced, as are many young women in these troubled times, with becoming an independent person and I felt, as women before me have felt, that I needed to fill that emptiness with a new challenge, to tackle an absorbing project that I could throw my whole self into. Several people had suggested that if I were ever in Florida I should contact Dick Shack, the agent who is so vitally involved in Anita Bryant's career. So while in Vero Beach working on an article for a flying magazine, I called his office. After speaking with him over the telephone, I decided to fly down to Miami to meet with him and discuss his ideas for developing a career as a performer. I remember well that January day in Miami. I had flown down and my "packaging" was absolutely wrong. In a wool suit (I had only winter clothes with me), I was roasting in the Florida sunshine. Stepping into the office I felt gawky, awkward, and shaky on the inside. On the outside I was trying desperately to sport the "Miss America smile" and the poise and confidence that go with it.

Sitting in his office I couldn't look over Mr. Shack's head at the clock on the wall or carry on an imaginary conversation with him. Fortunately Mr. Shack took over. All the tales about agents didn't match reality. No carnation in the lapel. No big black cigar, not even a cigarette. No glib, fast-paced dialogue. He seemed kind, interested, and very human. We talked of this and that—what I had done, what I could do, what I wanted to do—and I found myself forgetting my insecurity and relaxing into a real smile until he said, "How about singing?" That hit a very unconfident chord. I just couldn't bluff. If we were going to work together I had to be perfectly honest from the very beginning. Yes, I'd won a couple of vocalist awards in grade school and high school. I'd even won a scholarship in my freshman year in college for singing. And, of course, Kurley and I had sung together. But ventriloquism had to be my talent, I explained, because right after I was married I had had lung surgery. I hadn't sung since because I had no breath control.

"Ventriloquism," he said kindly, "is no longer really commercial in the top entertainment fields. Stay over a day and we'll go to a studio and make a tape of your voice."

When I got back to my empty apartment in California I felt the tape I had made was a disaster. All shaky notes and tones. And knees! So I was totally unprepared when, almost a month later, Mr. Shack called. "I think you've got a great potential. I played your tape for Chuck Bird, Anita Bryant's conductor, and he agreed. I think it would be worthwhile for you to come back to Miami and work with Chuck for a couple of weeks."

I returned to Miami to work with Chuck, but I don't think he was impressed with my ability as much as my ability to try.

From then on I'd fly to Miami for a week or more, work with Chuck eight or nine hours a day until we were both ready to drop, fly back to California, and practice by myself up to five hours a day. When I look back I'm sure it was my determination that encouraged Dick and Chuck and the others to work with me. I was giving it all I had because here was another impossible goal. Finally I faced my first audience as a professional singer.

I found immediately that there's a difference between audiences that you can actually feel. The audiences Kurley and I faced—the crowds that welcome Miss America, the church groups, the hometown folks who're rooting for you—were already pleased just because you're there. An audience that doesn't know you, to whom you're a total stranger, is there to be pleased. It sits totally impersonal waiting for you to make contact. You sense, too, that the press have become the critics—experts comparing you, not with some other college performer, but with some of the greatest talents that ever walked on stage. It's a very scary experience; it really is!

That first show I sang only four numbers and I didn't think I was going to get through it. If I'd never known what it was like to be nervous, now I got the full treatment. It's an awful feeling, choked, and shaky. I was on a show with people who'd been in show business a long time. They knew what to do. I didn't. I had a band behind me, which I'd never had before. I couldn't hear a word I was singing. I couldn't see the audience, and you can't sing a soft ballad to an invisible audience in long red underwear. My knees, under my long gown, had trembled so much they were actually weak when I walked off stage.

Mr. Shack said I'd done "a wonderful job," and I just shook my head. He said, "It was the best you could do for this time in your career. You got through it, and the audience liked it, no matter how nervous you were." I had to believe it for all I could think was, All that time, the breathing, the exercises, the vocalizing, the diction—just to feel miserable for those few minutes out there.

It was like starting all over again—but I wouldn't give up. It was like being so afraid I couldn't walk out on the stage. It was praying every time. "Help me get through what I'm going to do." This prayer helped me to say the words right, it helped me to try and get the notes right and to do my best. Again I knew I couldn't ask for any miracles. I had to do my best for where I was at that particular time, to go as far as my learning would take me.

My goal was to go on stage and each time do better than the time before. I was beginning to get a mental image of what I hoped to sound like, and every show I wanted to say, "This is the best show I've ever done." Only twice in a year's time did I have to say, "I didn't do better than I did last show."

With every performance I became better able to control my voice and my movements. I'd sound and move fine at rehearsals or in the studio when I was practicing. But still when I got on stage the whole thing seemed awkward. What was the trouble? Then I remembered, "To handle yourself, use your head—to handle others, use your heart." I was using my head to improve and master my technique. Now I would use my heart, too. Slowly I began working for audience reaction. I tried to make them understand the lyrics of my song. In doing this I got so involved with my song and the people in the audience that sometimes I completely forgot myself.

The real turning point came after one show when Mr. Shack asked me how a certain number, "Love is a Simple Thing," had gone. "That's funny," I said. "I know it went fine, but I don't remember anything I did during the song."

It was when I was singing and afterwards couldn't remember what I had done with my hands or how I had phrased the thoughts that I knew I had made real contact with the audience because what I did was natural and not contrived. There was not a *them* out there to be pleased, and a *me* up here going through a lot of studied sounds and gestures to please them. When I was open, vulnerable, without recourse to red underwear or alphabet smiles, the barriers were down and together we could communicate through music. It was then I knew that I had developed a confidence the old me didn't know I lacked.

It was then, too, I realized I held in my hand a most valuable key not only to unlock relationships with an audience but with any individual. *If you can begin to think about the other person you'll forget to worry about yourself.*

Soon I began sounding better, feeling better, looking better. I was more and more aware of my audiences, less and less aware of myself. And then it happened, my first earned standing ovation. I had introduced a new opening number to remind myself of my key—"Put a little love in your heart . . . think of your fellowman"—and when the audience looked deeper than the surface wrapping, the smile, the gown, the sounds, the gestures, they stood up and cheered. For they had at last found what I had hoped they would, what we are all looking for, that quality that draws us like a magnet. They had found someone who had finally really learned to *care*.

No Man Is a Stranger

Not long ago I attended the funeral of Dr. Richard E. Elvee. Dr. Elvee had been one of my first ministers, a close friend of my family, and it was before him that Andy and I recited our wedding vows. I came away from the funeral saddened, for we would all miss his living presence, but also uplifted by a tribute his son paid him on a memorial tape played at the service. He said, "It has been said that no man is an island. To my father no man was a stranger." He went on to tell how his father had always been at home in a bus depot, an airport, on a street corner. He was always at home with people in every place in the world.

I tried to imagine living in a world of men like that. Wouldn't it be wonderful to be that kind of person oneself?

I thought about the qualities that went to make up this universal man, who not only drew all kinds of people, was not only popular, but loved.

Dr. Elvee *cared,* no doubt about that. He cared for saint and sinner, young and old, lilies of the field and fallen sparrows. But the thing I remembered best about him was that his door was always open and he was always ready to *listen.*

I recall that Karl Menninger said, "When we're listened to, it creates us and makes us unfold." Friends and acquaintances who listen are those we will move toward. Today we have a veritable Grand Canyon of gaps: the Generation Gap, a gap between nations, between brother and brother, Christian and non-Christian, and, saddest of all, between Christian and Christian. It seems to me that a communication gap fosters all these divisions. Without communication there can be no contact, no relationship. We are always trying to bridge this gap—with our music, our poetry, our art, as well as the spoken and written word. But communication that isn't two way just isn't happening.

True communication takes an open mind, and an open ear, a respect for the spoken word or symbol on both sides in order to close the gaps. Hearing is a matter of vibrations on the eardrum. Listening is a matter of hearing with the heart. When we listen with our heart, then the mind goes on to know and understand another human being. Where there is true understanding there are no strangers. We may not agree, but we have a bridge upon which we can meet to work out our differences, a first step toward harmonious relationships.

Strangely enough, the people we find most attractive rarely do agree with us about everything. Our friends love us not because of our virtues (everyone does that), but in spite of our faults. And they care enough to help us handle those faults. It has been said, "A true friend doesn't sympathize with your weakness; instead he helps summon your strength."

I am thinking now of some people who, in the last few years, have helped me "summon my strength."

While working on the film *Hey There, Vonda* for Gospel Films, the company's president, Billy Zeoli, became a true friend and one of the most important spiritual guides and counselors I've ever known. Billy is an all-out successful businessman who, without saying a sanctimonious word, lets you know that he's plugged in to the heavenly power supply. I can always depend on him for an honest, straight-from-the-shoulder opinion. He's always there when you need him, and while I don't always like his advice, I usually know and find he's right, especially when it comes to spiritual matters.

Dick Shack always builds me up to myself and others. We all need a friend like that. When I make mistakes—and as my career began I made many—he has that wonderful quality of patience and the ability to somehow tell me I am wrong without hurting me. He had faith in me. That does a lot for anyone.

Another friend, Taris Savell, has been a tremendous help because she inspires me to think and create. A very talented gal, she can see the promise in one of my wild ideas and encourage me, or at times show me the bad points before I waste my time trying to make it into something workable.

Muriel and J. B. Sheets call me their adopted daughter and they have given me loving support through some difficult times and valuable friendship in good times. I can really let my hair down and relax with them. We all need people like that.

I truly believe that constructive criticism helps keep us from being strangers to ourselves as well as to others, that we should be big enough to take criticism or else we'll find we are too small to be praised—or loved.

On the other hand, self-criticism is usually very strong in us when we are young and insecure, and I think we have to be careful not to take to heart criticism we feel is undeserved. The opinions of others shouldn't discourage us from doing something we feel in our hearts is right and good. If we accept constructive criticism it strengthens us. If we accept destructive criticism, it can destroy not only our confidence, but ourselves.

Since I began my professional career I've had to learn to distinguish between the criticism that comes from understanding and caring, and the criticism that comes from misunderstanding and disapproval. And, strangely enough, all the misunderstanding and disapproval has come from a few of my fellow Christians.

Pop music is what I like, so that's what I sing. It moves in so many directions to say so many things that I feel it's the greatest way to communicate to the greatest number of people the things I have on my heart. When Kurley Q and I did our nostalgic appearance at the 50th Anniversary of the Miss America Pageant, we received countless wires and calls and letters from people in the secular and religious world congratulating us, especially from young people expressing joy at the way we represented them, thanking me for the books I've written, for the testimony I've been to them. The critics were more than kind. *The Hollywood Reporter* said: "Vonda Kay Van Dyke, Miss America of 1965, was a surprise hit of the evening in her production number. She displayed a fine voice and flair for musical comedy." *Variety* said: "Vonda Kay Van Dyke (1965) belted over a song buoyantly with (Bert) Parks, using her ventriloquist dummy." But from a Christian lady I received a stinging rebuke saying my performance had not glorified the Lord, and that, while she'd approved of my witness in the past, she really thought I was a hindrance now to the cause of Christ.

When I did some articles for *Christian Life,* I tried to bridge the Generation Gap by commenting on the new inspirational rock music and the new place this "joyful noise" has in today's America and today's church since it can communicate with young people in a way they can understand. The first "Letter to the Editor" I ever had in a magazine came from another Christian lady who had it on someone's authority that this was "an evil and pagan beat."

In a high-school auditorium where I sang some inspirational light rock in a show put on by the youth of the city yet another Christian lady took the trouble to tell me that I shouldn't be singing this kind of song in that kind of place.

If I am criticized, no matter how much it may hurt momentarily, my first reaction is, "Well, God love you, thank you for your concern." And that's from the heart. But then I have to make a decision. If I feel I am wrong, there have to be some changes made. If I feel I am right, I have to say, "I wouldn't be in this place singing this song in this way or writing this article if I thought it was wrong."

How do I decide who's right? I've found a little trick that helps me. It's not some voice from God, it's simply a matter of reaction. There are two ways in which most of us react to criticism. One is automatically to feel wronged, to take the defensive. If, when someone criticizes me, I immediately dislike and disagree with him without thinking about the things he's said, if I blindly say, "You're wrong; I'm right," then I put up a red flag that says, "Stop! Listen! Think!" This I have learned to do. I say to myself, "If you're so insecure after being criticized, that's a pretty good sign you're doing something wrong." But there are other times when someone criticizes me, and I'm quite happy about it. I don't take the defensive. I'm glad to hear his opinion, but I feel perfectly at peace with what I'm doing.

Recently I received a letter from a concerned Christian:

Dear Miss Van Dyke:
We were looking for your witness to Christ on TV the other night, but didn't see it.

We wondered if you still claim to be born again?

I am sure he and many others don't realize that on a major network television show, we are required to follow a prewritten script. With the exception of some of the current talk shows, I don't usually get an opportunity to witness or speak from my own heart and thoughts.

However, television exposure opens doors to other opportunities off camera. It seems that the more well known a performer becomes, the greater the impact of his witness is—especially among young people. I'm grateful for the concern shown in this letter but also aware of the misunderstanding that prompted it. No reason to get uptight and defensive.

Every Man Is a Friend

To go a step beyond the point where no man is a stranger, but every man is a friend, I think we would have to follow Dr. Elvee's special formula by giving Christian love to others.

Being involved with friends I've made in the entertainment business I've gained valuable insight into my own philosophy of life. Many don't believe in the same way that I do, but they have shown me that to profess to be a Christian, to go through the motions of making a commitment to Christ, is not enough. We have to put Christian love to work in our lives. I admire some of these people for their ability to act more like Christians than some of us professed Christians do.

Not long ago I wrote a letter to a friend who does not share all my beliefs but who sets a grand example of what a Christian should be. I wrote:

I like to be with you for many reasons, most of all because you have a lot of love in your heart, and you always let it show. You are concerned about others, what they need, what they think, what they expect, what they desire.

You are always warm to people and you freely show it in your smile, your thoughts, your words, and your feelings.

You are always considerate of your brother's philosophies, his ideals, and his personal beliefs. You are quick to try to understand the thoughts of others, and you readily attempt to capture their interpretations and meaning to words and situations.

You are honest in your appraisal of yourself and *in the appraisal of others, and your honesty has the ability to be gentle and sparing with your criticism and abundant with your praise.*

You simply live *the "Golden Rule"—a person can have no finer quality than this.*

As I wrote, I thought, I wish I could begin to live up to those ideals myself. The Golden Rule is a basic for Christian love. And Dr. Elvee's life had proved that genuine love (Christian love as Christ described it) has a special kind of magnetism which draws people much as water draws a thirsty man to a fountain. If all we Christians could constantly radiate just a little of the love we receive from God, the Father, we might indeed see the brotherhood of man on earth.

8

Happy Together

Recently, I sang on a Kraft Music Hall. After my number, Bert Parks joined me in singing "Happy Together." Many remarked how "happy together" we did sing. (We were, we really had fun!) Bert is one of my friends who has that special something called charisma. His secret seems to be his desire to make the other person look good. Being less concerned about himself and seemingly more concerned about you spells instant rapport. He seems to live a lesson in successful friendship. If we learn to think of the other person, that can be a major contributing factor to "happy togetherness" in an even more serious relationship.

In all the books I've read (and written), discussions of dating days take precedent over discussions of marriage. This would seem to be logical since they indubitably happen first.

But is it?

One of the things I know now is that most of the questions I'm asked concerning those important, exciting years when boys and girls are beginning to discover each other as young adults could be answered by them individually *if their goal was clear.*

If the end point of our dating days is a happy marriage we need to know how to prepare for a happy marriage. If we realize in the beginning that giving ourselves completely, without reservation, to a mate is the second most important commitment we'll ever have a chance to make, the answers to our dating problems will come clear at the time the questions arise. We'll be aware that our future happiness will be determined by our now decisions, which is the best guide we can have.

What do we need to know to reach toward a real, lasting love and a real, lasting marriage?

Love and Marriage

It is a foregone conclusion in our culture as well as our favorite fairy tales, fiction, and films that, as the old song says, "love and marriage go together like a horse and carriage." Therefore, the first question that comes to us is, "How do you know if you're really in love?"

My favorite answer is, "When you stop asking, you know."

But as we're growing into this mature experience, as we're learning to relate, learning what we like and admire in others and they in us, slowly forming that mental picture of the kind of person we'd want to live with for the rest of our lives, we can experience very strong emotions that seem to us like the real thing. Some are beautiful, sincere, valuable at that time and stage of our development. Some are agonizing. Some are dangerous. The Irish playwright George Bernard Shaw said, "First love is only a little foolishness and a lot of curiosity." The wit of the cynic is strictly on the negative side, but there is a truth here that can help us. Because, if we don't keep our goal in view, when we begin to experience those first genuine emotional attractions, there can be a lot of foolishness as well as curiosity in our relationships. And that's dangerous.

There is a danger, too, in fantasy attachments. We want to love someone. We have dreams, and affection to give, and no one yet in sight to share them. So we create a love object, either by building up someone we already know, or even someone we don't know at all. Youth today, with its freedom and frankness, its ability to form meaningful attachments with the opposite sex without romantic attachment, seems less vulnerable to this form of loneliness than in my own dating days. But the situation still does exist, as any victim of the superfan brigade can attest. During my Miss America year I not only received serious proposals of marriage by mail from total strangers (all of which went unanswered), but also a valuable diamond engagement and wedding ring in an envelope with a six-cent stamp on it and another diamond on my doorstep at Christmas (all of which were returned without comment). One unidentified gentleman, along with his pet parakeet, arrived in Phoenix by bus to announce that he was my "intended."

They sound like kooks, don't they? But to an adult who has encountered the authentic marriage relationship it doesn't seem any kookier than when young people who have just "fallen in love" think they know each other well enough to make even the smallest commitment.

A quote I think all young people, male and female, should engrave on their memories for sound emotional guidance as well as good thoughts comes from F. Alexander Magoun. "Love develops slowly, for it is a capacity requiring growth. It cannot spring full blown at first sight, as infatuation can."

When "packaging" meets "packaging," when romantic meets romantic, when loneliness reaches out for love, when those first physiological stirrings arouse answering emotions in another, it can strike a spark that will ignite a bonfire—and we may call it love. But unless we wait to see whether a deeper relationship will be kindled the smoke will definitely get in our eyes, and we can be left with nothing but ashes and tears. If we take our time, use our heads as well as our hearts, realize that we are undergoing one of the greatest and most meaningful transitions that we'll make in this lifetime, we can enjoy what is beautiful, avoid what is dangerous, and be moving securely toward our major goal.

Before making a final decision on any guy or gal, instead of asking someone else if we're really in love, we should be able to answer these questions for ourselves.

1   Do we have common ideals and tastes?
2   Is there a willingness to give and take?
3   Is the desire to be with him or her a strong one?
4   Is there always a readiness to *listen* and consider the other's opinion?
5   Do we feel there's never enough time to be together?
6   Have we pride and respect? Do we have to apologize for any reason?
7   Can we disagree and remain agreeable?
8   Is there absolute faith and trust?
9   Do we think in terms of two, not just one?
10 Is the other's company more important than anyone else's?
11 Do you want to please him or her, even if it means giving up your own way?
12 Does the other bring out the best in you?
13 Does he or she really turn us on?

If you can answer yes to these questions, my mirror says you may really be in love. But now we come to a question that no one has ever asked me, one I think is equally as important as the first, but we don't know enough to ask it. Is it a foregone conclusion that real love will automatically lead to a real and lasting marriage? I think this assumption is one of the greatest myths with which our culture deludes young people. For my answer would be no!

Are You Ready for This?

I believe that when you find you're really in love you then have grounds for going steady or becoming engaged. I also believe strongly in a period of engagement and I do *not* mean trial marriage. A trial marriage, by whatever name you call it, is an unreal situation and doesn't prove a thing. If unsuccessful it only dims or demolishes our chances of making a success of the reality.

I've joked a lot about marriage and said that the first year you learn everything that you don't like about each other. The second year you begin to find there are some things you do like about each other. But marriage is no joke. And the engagement period is a much better time for finding out these things than after you've made a permanent commitment.

How long? Until you've given yourselves time to answer a lot more questions about each other. There are things that could and should be discussed *before* marriage, compromises to be reached, agreements sought. Discussions before marriage aren't arguments, they're not a panic situation. If you find areas where you can't agree, things you can't live with, breaking off the engagement is the right and proper thing to do. If you find them after you've taken your vows—what then?

You should know everything you possibly can about the person you intend to marry, and he about you. Even the "little things" can become unbelievably "big" on a daily basis. Does one of you like to go out every night? Does the other prefer to stay home? Is one of you meticulous and the other not? You're not going to be roommates learning to live and let live for one semester. You're aiming at being together for a lifetime. Do you really like the same things? Silly as it seems, to disagree on every kind of food can make life difficult. What about activities? When you're first in love there never *is* enough time to be together. But to leap into marriage only to find that the wife is tied up every night with church and community activities and the husband vanishes to the golf course every weekend shatters togetherness pretty abruptly if the husband can barely tolerate her involvement and the wife hates his golf. Somehow if these things come as surprises *after* the wedding day—"You didn't tell me . . ." one said. "You never asked," replied the other. "She never said . . ."—this initiates a great deal of resentment. In order to handle these things harmoniously, we need to face them before the situation arises.

This takes time. It's unwise, even dangerous, to assume anything. Even after we've had discussions, we need to see if the most sincere words are borne out in conduct. This takes more time. It takes time even to think of all the things that need to be discussed. But there are major areas in which, if we stop to think about it, we already know an understanding must be reached if we are to convert a beautiful romance into a forever marriage. One other thing we need to remember. Marriage has been called an institution—but it is not a reformatory. It is equally dangerous and unwise to assume that the state of matrimony is going to make drastic, or even promised, changes in the other person. So we have to try and see it like it is, without rose-colored glasses. If promises are made they should be confirmed in action.

What are the major areas that should be explored?

To me the top priority is your philosophy of life. Since this is the basis for our character, our decisions, our highest ideals and goals, if our philosophies are not compatible it's going to be very difficult to be "happy together." If you have found, as I have, that the first and greatest commitment you have a chance to make is to Christ and that the one you intend to marry has not made this same commitment, then you can never really share the deepest things in your heart. You can't assume the other person believes as you do because you met in a certain place or because someone else told you he does. The best way to find out what another person believes is to ask point blank. Then discuss it in depth. Then see how they live it.

Today, with women already so liberated, it is very necessary for an engaged couple to have a clear picture of what the husband expects of his wife—whether his image includes her completing college, having a career, or whether he just assumes that she will leave at the altar every dream except "occupation: housewife." This, as in all other areas, is a matter for personal agreement. There is no right or wrong to it. It's simply a question of having a frank, open discussion to see if you can arrive at a *mutually* agreeable solution. In my own case Andy was completely in accord with me continuing my activities. Fortunately we explored it down to the last detail—the use of my maiden name professionally. "Fine," he said. "Use Vonda Kay Van Dyke professionally and Mrs. Laird at home. I have no objection whatsoever." He proved it the first time someone came up to us and said, "Hello, Mr. Van Dyke." Without batting an eyelash he said, "Excuse me, it's Doctor."

Discussing money is important because it can be the cause of much friction. If both of you are earning, how will you work out the details of paying bills, savings, and spending money? If a wife, as she so often does these days, is working to help her husband get his college degree, his masters or Ph.D., who will have to handle the finances? If her occupation is housewife, will there be any money that she can call her own? In discussing money your philosophy of life may enter in. Many Christians, myself included, believe in tithing. I personally think I should give God a portion of everything I make, since it is by His Grace that I make anything at all. Some people believe in giving a lot, some a little, some nothing. Many believe in supporting churches or charitable organizations. Others think their taxes should do the job. I believe all these things should be worked out mutually before you are in the marriage situation. I believe, too, that people have different *attitudes* toward money. Some are frugal; some extravagant. You can observe the differences. If a girl who doesn't make much spends a great deal on clothes while her fiancé who does make a great deal always takes her to a hamburger joint, it's time to talk.

Another place where observation helps is in the classic in-law situation. I think it's a great thing for both to get to know their prospective in-laws. This can promote understanding and help avoid more friction. It can also serve another purpose. Most parents are not pushing their child off into marriage. They're a little reluctant about it. When they're reluctant, whether they realize it or not, they'll tell you negative things about this dear child of theirs you're going to marry. Don't just brush it off. Listen to them, and check it out. Some of the things that come out by accident may have a lot to do with how you get along later.

One of the truly vital areas to explore concerns your individual family. Do you or do you not want children? If so, how many? Do you believe in planned parenthood? Do you think you should wait to have your family until you have firmly established your personal relationship? Do you think it helps to establish that relationship to have your children immediately?

Here conflicting philosophies of life can create havoc. But so can all the free advice you get from the economists, the ecologists, the psychologists, counselors, lecturers—and all your friends and relations. Each has an answer for you. Yet this is perhaps the most private, personal area of all. Forgetting all others, I think it must be thoughtfully discussed and mutually agreed upon by the engaged couple themselves.

If I have put very little of myself into this chapter it is because I truly believe, despite all evidences we hear and read to the contrary, that marriage itself should be a very personal, private affair. A real, lasting love and a real lasting marriage are experienced by two unique individuals.

I have shared with you my thoughts on the best way to steer your course through your dating days toward that goal. But now I would like to add one personal word. The best marriage insurance I know of would be for *both* husband and wife to ask God into the relationship. Then marriage becomes, not an institution, but a sacrament.

That very wise minister Louis H. Evans said, "Many a marriage could have been saved if the couple had remembered this: that their hearts belong to each other, but their souls belong to God!"

But this, too, must be mutually agreed upon if they are to be happy together.

9

It's Our World

One Christmas Eve, three American astronauts caught up with science fiction and became the first human beings to orbit the moon. As Apollo 8 and her three weightless explorers circled within seventy miles of that mysterious surface, one of her crew sent a significant message back over the eerie empty miles.

As he was swept through the "vast loneliness here on the moon" Capt. James A. Lovell Jr., said, "It's awe-inspiring and it makes you realize just what you have back there on earth. The earth from here is a grand oasis in the great vastness of space."

Columbus once sailed into the unknown to seek a new route to India and instead discovered a "new world." The astronauts who had penetrated 231,000 miles into outer space to see for the first time the further side of the moon looked back and discovered—earth!

I myself believe this message had a lasting impact, consciously or unconsciously, on every young person on our planet. Interested as we are in the scientific marvels of our age—atomic power, cybernetics, space exploration—I don't think any generation before ours has been more aware of this "grand oasis," of what we have here and how good it is, nor more determined to defend, preserve, and improve it.

Your concerns and your involvements cover such a wide range that it would take another book to talk about them all. But here let's take a look at a few.

Flower Power, Sole Power, and You

In *Ecotactics: the Sierra Club Handbook for Environment Activists,* Peter R. Janssen writes:

> *Since Woodstock, many American students have come to believe that they are entering a peaceful, loving, brotherhooding Age of Aquarius, in which the sound of music (rock, of course) shall be heard again in our land. But within this questing movement, tens of thousands of young people have turned their own love toward the earth in an effort to repair ravished landscapes, oil-filled harbors and over-crowded cities, to patch the gaping holes in the quality of modern life. For them, this is the Age of Ecology.*

With ecology, flower power has grown up.

If we add to this love of earth a tremendous concern for "brotherhooding," I think we have a true picture of our most vital interests. It is here that the majority of young people have already begun to show imaginative, creative leadership and have made a positive contribution toward a better, happier world.

In my travels I am continually amazed and encouraged by the young people I've come in contact with. The vast majority are sincere, sensitive, honest, enthusiastic about—and interested in —life. And they are showing their concern. These are the cream of the crop—the kids I love to be around.

I've spotted these outstanding young people within the framework of many of the great youth organizations I've worked with, and I've met them on campuses all over the country. They are fantastic! It's encouraging to see the endless ambition and determinatiton of the 4H'ers involved in competitions that might lead them to a college scholarship. It's gratifying to view the fresh enthusiasm of a fellow or gal involved in Youth for Christ trying to explain to a discouraged classmate that God really does care about him. It's inspiring to see the satisfaction written on the face of a tired teen-ager, drudging the last mile of his hike for hunger and knowing that the few cents per mile that someone is paying him will perhaps save the life of a brother. It's exciting to hear the united cry of a young generation that seems to care about the world, who study ecology and worry about pollution and do something about it. It's a feeling of deep pride to know the kids who aren't walking around in circles and in crowds, carrying meaningless signs and shouting impossible demands; instead, they are breaking out on their own, using their alert minds to learn and discover new ways to solve their problems. They're not wasting their time at sit-ins. They're on their feet, willing and ready to work for solutions. If you're one of these youths who care and are aware, congratulations!

Tune In, Turn On, and Fly!

What do I think of kids and drugs?

I think you ask me this question as often as older people do because you feel that combination represents one of the most negative, destructive threats to your collective future, for when I turn the tables and ask you what *you* think most of you say flatly, "Drugs are a cop-out." The intelligent, informed people I've met are "in their right minds" and propose to stay there. They recognize that "experimenting" with drugs is about on a par with "experimenting" with bombs. They wouldn't be caught dead messing with either because they are well aware that this is an exact statement of calculated risk—being "caught dead"— either mentally, with a mind blown beyond repair, or physically, with a shattered body, or both.

What then attracts some unwary to drugs? Users insist that drugs "expand their minds," give them a new perspective of themselves and the world. Even at the risk of insanity they get "high" above the mundane world on "trips," some good, some unbelievably bad, into an unpredictable fantasy land.

I find it strange that many of the same young people who are determined to uncover "hypocrisy" and devaluate "myths" can deceive themselves with a phony, synthetic, chemical experience. What's the good of a "new perspective" of what isn't so to begin with? I can see why some of their friends feel that they are copping-out if they use drugs to escape into unreality. The best solution, it seems to me, would be to show them how to encounter the real thing, the natural, genuine mind-expanding experiences with which the real world abounds.

I, myself, along with thousands of young people, have discovered an authentic "high." A small dose is guaranteed to give you a thrill, and while it's known to be habit-forming, the lasting effects are demonstrably beneficial. On these trips you'll get a genuine new perspective not only of yourself but, like the astronauts, of the vast sky and the grand earth. This "high" is a literal one, starting from the ground up.

At the age of five I remember wanting to go all alone to "the other side of a cloud." A few years ago, with the encouragement of my husband who holds a commercial license and an instrument rating, I took up flying—and went. And from the other side of the cloud, on and on, I've found wonder after wonder. My first long solo flight was from Long Beach to Phoenix over nothing but mountains and deserts. In flight, all by myself up there, I was tickled. It was a wild feeling to know I was up in the sky, just hanging there. Nobody below, nobody above that I could see. The radio was quiet and all I could hear was the steady hum of the engine. I remember praying out loud, "Boy, isn't this fantastic! Why didn't You let me know about this sooner? Thank You for creating something like this world and giving me a chance to see it like I'm seeing it today."

A great many young people, male and female, are getting their flying licenses as early as the law allows; their solo license on their sixteenth birthday, their private license on their seventeenth, and some even go on to get their commercial ticket when they turn eighteen. The cost is not prohibitive and, when we compare log books, we're agreed that every hour is worth it, not only for practical purposes, like getting you from here to there, or even the pleasure of "turning on" your friends with your new accomplishment, but for the most radiant feature attraction in the world of aviation, an *encounter with beauty*. To actually slide across miles of powder blue silk, edged in lace and trimmed with snowy white fur; to be engulfed in a collage of clouds and colors, rose, pink, violet, yellow, orange; to be suspended like a star in the black velvet of night—this is to be part of a beauty beyond the earth-bound or drug-induced imagination. Is there a surer way to get a newer, truer perspective of yourself and the world than when you're engulfed by the expansive silence of a quiet sky, contemplating, meditating, feeling almost like a part of the universe itself?

So when I'm asked what to do about the drug scene, beyond seeing that young people are fully informed of the dangers, I have to say, on the positive side, "God and man have combined efforts to provide so many real, wonderful things for us to enjoy. Flying is only one of them. So why not explore them? Find out 'high' in reality, naturally, so we can be sure it will expand our consciousness and not destroy it."

God offers to everyone His special formula for an exciting life of reality which provides us with the power to face each day with confidence. All we have to do is accept and apply His formula to our lives.

In the *Look* article "The Jesus Movement Is Upon Us," a young girl is quoted. "I am stoned. I'm stoned on Jesus. Only it's far better than being stoned. Drugs are a 'down.' This is the most incredible 'up' in the world. I feel like I'm floating all the time with Jesus."

I Lead Nine Lives

It is, I suppose, natural that I get a lot of questions about woman's place in the world today. Because women's attitudes and conduct are a vital force, influencing not only men and children but our entire culture, this question is of concern to both sexes. Unfortunately the current focus is on a small group, the so-called feminist movement, which is calling attention to itself by various demonstrations.

What the members are demonstrating, or what they are demonstrating against, they have yet to make entirely clear to me.

If, in the name of women's lib, they're asking for equal pay for women doing equal jobs equally as well as men, then I'm all for them. They're simply an extension of those pioneers who won us the right to wear bloomers instead of steel corsets, to receive higher education, to own property, to vote. This I call progress. But some of the fringe benefits they seem to be demanding don't seem like benefits to me. I don't think the right to look unattractive, to assume a man's role, to let him take over my apron or my kitchen, is either a great privilege or progress. Nor, if I understand them correctly, would I feel more liberated or happier if men would kindly cease to open doors for me, permit me to carry my own heavy packages, and pay me the courtesy of not admiring me or my best new dress. However, as far as I know, if that's the way they want it, there's no law on the books that says they can't have it that way, but they don't have to protest. It's a matter of choice.

It seems to me as I watch this aggressive fight for these so-called rights that some girls aren't demonstrating for femininity, but against it; that if they get what they're asking for they may well lose the greatest and only unique right a woman has—the right to be feminine. When I'm brought face to face with them on television shows they seem to be demonstrating their own insecurity as women, and that makes me an unfair judge.

I feel very secure as a female. I don't remember ever wanting to be a boy. I still don't. I like being feminine and so do the vast majority of women with whom I come in contact.

Actually, there has never been a generation where a girl has had so many opportunities to fulfill herself in so many ways of her own choosing. She can stay single without the old-fashioned stigma of "old maid." She can have all the education she can take. She is eligible for scholarships. (I find it interesting that the Miss America pageant which called forth a "feminists" demonstration in past years, is the largest scholarship foundation for women in the world.) She can go as far in her career as her ability will take her, combine it with marriage and a family if she chooses. If she decides against a career and for being a full-time housewife, she still has the whole world of sport open to her, plus creative involvement in community, church, social, and volunteer organizations. She can dedicate her creativity strictly to her home, to its furnishings, her cooking, her garden, her sewing machine, and be a winner. She can have any, or all, of these experiences, putting them together in the combination her desires dictate.

It seems to me the real danger to modern woman is not that she has too few opportunities to become a person, but too many. Unless a firm central core, like the hub of a wheel, holds her activities together, she may succumb to what William James described in the German word, *Zerrissenheit,* "torn-to-pieces-hood."

I, myself, feel I lead all at one time as many lives as the proverbial cat. I am a housewife. I have a career as a singer. I compose music. I write—columns, articles, books, even poetry. I fly. I play golf. I snorkle and water ski. I recently started a small art collection—and someday I'd like to study painting and learn to play the guitar. I have friends and family with whom I want to spend time. And, of course, at the center I have my faith in God and the many opportunities that come for me to share my thoughts with you.

How, I am asked, do I do it all?

It's really simple. No matter what I'm doing, I'm not "switching hats," playing different roles. If I were, I'd get so confused I couldn't do it. My central core is that I'm a person, and that "me" is a woman. I have not time nor energy to waste protesting or demonstrating. I have affirmed and accepted myself as an individual—and also as a woman. I don't worry about being equal—or superior—or inferior to men. I enjoy being "me." I feel that whatever attributes or qualities I have come through in all my activities. This is where it's at. If we've got intelligence, special qualities, and talents, we don't have to broadcast them. They will be noticed.

I think to affirm who I am and what I am is the way to live creatively, the way to fulfill myself. From what I've seen, despite the negative protestors who make news with their demonstrations, ours is an affirmative generation. We are affirming ourselves—and life—all of it. As in one of the songs I like to sing:

> It's my world and it's your world, too.
> There's an awful lot we both can do
> If we try.

10

Troubled Waters

Someone once said about me, "If you put her in hell she'd probably look around and say, 'Gee, what a lovely fire!' " Well, I'll never have to test that statement, thanks to the Lord. But it is true that I tend to remember and dwell on the good things and dismiss the bad ones.

It is not true, however, that I do not have deeply troubled moments. At times those inner hurts, discouragement, disappointment, fear, tragedy—the sort of problems for which we have no personal explanation or solution—threaten to overwhelm us all. Some of them we can share, some are too deeply personal and we'd rather keep them to ourselves. But we all have these moments and it's important to learn how to deal with them.

So far I've found that, if I can search out my particular talents, uncover my unique personality, learn to set my goal, make effective choices, affirm myself and my relationship to the world, I can lead a happier, more meaningful life.

When it comes to really troubled waters I personally have found no bridge across except prayer, no haven except my faith in God.

Like everyone else I've been upset to the point of tears with that jumbled up feeling inside of close to hopelessness and complete helplessness. When this happens I remember to pray for

God's peace. It's even hard for me to understand how God can make me feel His calmness and joy and the relief of His promised presence while the teardrops are still wet on my face. There's a feeling of wonder that I can't explain. It's really "something else"! No matter what some who have not *had* the experience may say, feeling His presence at times like that is not a form of rationalization. It's not positive thinking or simply a distraction from negative thinking.

He is really there!

When I am in difficulty, I turn, over and over again, to two scriptural references in *Living Letters*. "We are pressed on every side by troubles, but not crushed or broken. We are perplexed because we don't know why things happen as they do, but we don't give up and quit. We are hunted down, but God never abandons us. We get knocked down, but we get up again and keep going" (II Corinthians 4:8-9).

And, ". . . the more you suffer, the more God will bless you, and help you, and give you His joy" (II Corinthians 1:7).

It's hard to believe that this is so until you've proven it for yourself. But looking back over my life so far, I realize that I have profited greatly by being crushed under the load of troubles. I've never really welcomed them at the time but I can see now that with each set of problems that are pushed upon me I become more flexible. Each time I seem to crumble inside under the weight of them, God, in His wonderful way, reaches down during my weakest moments and patches me up, remolding me, making me into someone stronger than I was before—if I turn to Him in prayer.

I have learned to pray by praying. Prayer is my conscious contact with the Source of help. And my difficult times certainly encourage me to keep that line open. But if we haven't learned to make the contact, or if we've let it become just a habit of repeating words, it may be difficult to get through to the Living Presence in an emergency.

In our home when I was young, my mother and father and I prayed before meals, and I said my prayers at bedtime. I always thought I had to tell everything in the world to God before I went to sleep—catch Him up on the news, my needs, make petitions for all my friends and relations. Then I heard of a great Christian leader who, when day was done, didn't kneel down or say any prayers. He just climbed into bed, pulled up the covers, and said, "Good night, God." Obviously he had been conversing with Him all day long, while things were happening, so all he had left to say at bedtime was "Good night." This so impressed me that my own prayers ceased to be a ritual or habit and I began to practice trying to be aware of His presence all day long.

If I was filled with joy, as I was on that magnificent solo flight, I found myself making impromptu prayers of praise and gratitude. If I was troubled I asked for help right now. I found that when I could do this I had a constant Companion, as well as Comforter.

During my Miss America year I developed a fear, not of people, but of crowds. Just after my reign began we were making some pictures in a warehouse in New York and when we came out a large group of kids were waiting. I was happy to meet them but as they converged on me they began pulling at my clothes, ripping off little pieces for souvenirs. I panicked and ran for the car. It happened again at the stage door after the Ed Sullivan Show. "You'll just have to get used to it," I was told, "because that's the way it will be." I can't say I ever got used to it, but I found that, by casting my burden on the Lord, trusting Him to be with me, I was able to walk smiling and unafraid through those crowds.

For me He is the Comforter in a very real sense. When I was in high school I faced deep tragedy for the first time. A singing group, including students from our school, drove to California to perform. On their way back their car hit a bridge and three of them, including Chuck, a great guy who was dating my next door neighbor, and a close girl friend of mine, were killed instantly. These sudden deaths stunned us all. It was up to me to comfort Chuck's girl friend—the first time I had ever tried to comfort anyone. I did a lot of praying and then tried to explain to her that, while we were both going to miss them, because they were Christians, Chuck and the other two were happy. I was trying to convince myself, too. Then we went to the funerals, and I was convinced. The Comforter was *there*.

In this situation it wasn't easier only because I was a Christian but because they too were Christians—I knew that they had a place with God, that they were happy, and that I was going to see them again. Talking it over afterward, we who had been their friends agreed that this was one of the greatest blessings of our Christian faith. There were no permanent separations and it offered us eternal happiness.

When some years later I myself faced major surgery the possibility was there that I might die, but I really wasn't afraid. I was a little apprehensive at first but I prayed about it. He was with me, and I was at peace.

And so, even in troubles, I've learned to try to rejoice. Paul had the right idea: "What a wonderful God we have—He is the Father of our Lord Jesus Christ, the source of every mercy, and the One Who so wonderfully comforts and strengthens us in our hardships and trials. And why does He do this? That when others are troubled, needing our sympathy and encouragement, we can pass on to them this same help and comfort God has given us" (II Corinthians 1:3-4 LL).

11

The Sign of the Fish

My first trip to Japan was at Easter time. The country was colorful with cherry blossoms, and cloth fish were fluttering from the flagpoles outside many houses. These fish told the passing world how many male children had been born into the family. I knew that the sign of the fish had another meaning.

Two thousand years ago when a small band of early Christians were eagerly spreading the Good News at the risk of their lives, there was a secret sign by which Christ's followers identified themselves to one another. A crude drawing of a fish, now called a *mandorla,* appeared on doorways, outside of shops, on the walls of the catacombs. This cryptic symbol for Christ referred to the fact that the letters in the Greek word for fish, *ichthus,* served as initials for the words Jesus Christ, Son of God, Saviour. Today the sign is appearing again—painted by young people on their minibuses, ornamenting their art, cast in silver and hung from chains around their necks.

Because in this one chapter I want to speak directly to my young Christian friends, I am doing it under the "sign of the fish" so that we can identify one another. The things we have to talk about are the self-same things that bound the early Christians together and those who have no interest may wish to bypass this intimate discussion.

Meaningful Worship

While living in Los Angeles I used to attend Bel Air Presbyterian Church. A three-time all-American football player by the name of Donn Moomaw is the pastor. I have borrowed a portion of one of his sermon outlines describing meaningful worship.

The tradition of sameness of Sunday morning service—do you begin to think of this as your little security blanket? Or does worship mean more than that to you? Does it mean a reaching out—a searching for reality—a chance to praise and learn?

In other words, are we really Christians who are finding our true answers and meaning for today in Jesus Christ? Or are we just nice people who, through choice or habit, find it pleasant to spend our Sunday mornings in church?

These seem to me to be very important questions for those of us who accept the identity of Christians to ask ourselves. I believe that all of us would like to have our worship meaningful, and if we find it is not, there is a way to make it so.

Meaningful worship begins simply with an awareness of God. It's our awareness of God that's significant rather than a creed, denomination, minister, or boy friend or girl friend who goes to the same church. After becoming aware of God we not only need to become aware of His Son, Jesus Christ, but we must *accept* Him. Scripture puts this very plainly. In order to know and accept Christ we must recognize our sins, ask for forgiveness, and *believe*. Belief and trust are referred to so emphatically in the New Testament, yet there are many trying to give their worship meaning without them.

I heard Bill Glass use an illustration once about his son. "What does the word trust mean, daddy? How do you have faith?" Bill said, "Stand up on the stairway there." Then he turned out the lights and said, "Okay, son, jump into your daddy's arms." Without hesitation the little boy jumped because he knew his father would catch him. That's what faith is—and trust. It's not having to see: it's letting go and loving God. This is what receiving Him means.

In order to know Him, to have faith, and in turn have a meaningful worship, it's important that we be humble. It says again and again in Scripture that proud people don't find God. Someone once said, "A proud man looks down at people and things, and looking down, can't look up." So there's a particular attitude that we need when we go to church on Sunday. It's an attitude of looking *up*—expecting to receive.

If we're so busy looking *around*—to see what others are doing or not doing—or looking *down* to disagree or criticize, we're actually rejecting the One who said, "A new commandment I give you: love one another. . . . If you have love for one another, then all will know that you are my disciples" (John 13:34 TEV).

This I had to find out for myself.

When I was in high school my parents changed churches and I was very upset. I wasn't in favor of the new church because it wasn't what I was used to. The young people did things I objected to, the teachers said things I didn't agree with, I became so negative that I didn't want to go to church on Sunday. I was suffering from what I now know is called *spiritual* pride, looking down on the people around me and saying to myself, *"They* don't know what religion is all about!"

In later years when young people asked me if I have ever been criticized for my beliefs, I have said honestly that I have never been criticized by non-believers because they generally accept me as sincere. I have only been criticized by Christians, which does seem a shame. But I could also tell them from my own experience that this lack of love in others, while it stings, can't really damage us, but the lack of love in ourselves can. For when I was proud I was looking down so much that I wasn't looking *up* at all. I had cut *myself* off from meaningful worship.

Fortunately I could discuss my feelings quite openly with my parents. I said frankly, "I don't want to be a part of this." And they wisely guided me in a positive direction. They said, "Instead of just criticizing the things you don't agree with why don't you see if you can't help to make their faith more vital? Get involved in the leadership of the group?"

I did just that, but to do it I had to look to God for guidance. And as I became involved I found young people just as eager as I to help the others find faith as a reality, to show them that Sunday church wasn't something to joke about but could be the most stimulating, helpful event of our week.

I thought if they weren't discovering what faith was, if they were lukewarm or socializing or coming on Sunday just because their parents brought them, the place to start was with the younger children. From that day right up to the Miss America Pageant every summer I taught a Sunday school class in that church. The summer before the pageant was a busy one—there were my Miss Arizona appearances, work to be done on my wardrobe, in modeling classes and the health studio, with Kurley at Legend City, on my quotations—but my Sunday school class had become a revitalizing part of my life. That particular summer I taught juniors in high school and I learned as much as my class did. We talked about the lessons in a very free manner, discussed the Christian life in today's crazy world and developed a real friendship that helped us all to go out and live it more fully. I heard the other day that the definition of religion is to reunite and I found that this was true. The real meaning of religion is to reunite yourself with God and with His people.

The greatest feeling of humility came when I was seated at my church homecoming dinner after the Miss America Pageant. Two young men from that summer class got up and said that because of it they had decided to enter the ministry. I wondered then how I could ever have been so proud. Because I had humbled myself to look up to God's guidance, I had a reward that was really quite intangible. But there was a tangible reward, too, for during my Miss America year I was continually amazed at the inspiration I received when I visited different churches. I was in worship services of all denominations, with all kinds of music, all kinds of buildings, all kinds of ministers. But I never left a Sunday morning service without having received something strong—something that was going to be really meaningful to me and for me.

I had learned the value of that attitude of humility, so every Sunday I went looking *up,* knowing *God* would provide the message I needed. It was the feeling of expectancy, the positive attitude that did it. If you expect to receive something from God—you will!

But what we receive has to be expressed in our lives if Sunday worship is to be truly meaningful. It's not enough either to just revolve around our own little Christian circle. It's doing what those early Christians did, as Donn Moomaw put it, "making a marriage between work and worship, between the sacred and the secular." How do we do this?

The first thing we need to do is give time to God—not just in church or on Sunday. It's spending time with Him in prayer, reading His Word.

A few years ago I spent a day with one of Billy Zeoli's sons. He was then seven years old. Steven is a handsome young man and when I told him so he grinned and grinned. Later he told his father, "Gee, she really likes me. She likes my blue eyes and she thinks I'm going to be handsome when I grow up." His father wisely said, "Son, that means she likes you on the outside. It doesn't mean she likes you on the inside." Steven thought this over and said, "Dad, she likes me on the inside, too." "How do you know?" his father asked. "Because," replied Steve, "she gives time to me!"

This is how we show love for God—by giving Him our lives, our time. As we read our Scripture, as we continually ask His help and guidance in prayer, we can close the gap between our worship and our daily lives by *living* as nearly as we can the way He wants us to.

In my copy of *Living Letters* there are a few verses in Romans 12 which I have marked "How to be a tip-top Christian in living." As often as I re-read them I'm aware that all too frequently I fall short of the tip-top, but they keep the goal before me.

> Don't just pretend that you love others: really love them. Hate what is wrong. Stand on the side of the good.
> Love each other with brotherly affection and delight to honor each other.
> Never be lazy in your work but serve the Lord enthusiastically.
> Be glad for all God is planning for you. Be patient in trouble, and prayerful always.
> Never pay back evil for evil. Do things in such a way that everyone can see you are honest clear through.
> Don't quarrel with anyone. Be at peace with everyone just as much as you possibly can.
> Don't let evil get the upper hand but conquer evil by doing good.
> (Romans 12:9-12, 17, 18, 21)

In every day reality this simply means giving to others the love that Christ gives us. It means standing up for our principles even when there's no one to stand with us. It means taking a lower grade on a test because we won't cheat even if everyone else does. It means that, since we've taken the path to become part of the *sacred* world, the "kingdom of God," by accepting His Son, if we believe strongly enough and reach steadily toward our goal of tip-top Christian living, we can walk the broad highways of the *secular* world, among those who don't know Him, securely and without straying.

In making God and our faith an everyday reality we bring the sacred and secular together and translate joyful, meaningful worship into joyful, meaningful lives.

If we are finding this difficult we need to go back over the steps and take each one thoroughly. We need to prepare ourselves for worship by our awareness of God, by accepting God's Son. We must be humble and expectant. We must give time to God. And we must, through our daily actions, show the reality of our faith. Then we, too, are ready to pass the Good News on to others.

"Happiness Is Knowing the Lord!"

One of the most joyous aspects of our Christian experience is our opportunity to tell others what we've found. Sometimes it's hard to restrain our enthusiasm in witnessing for Him but in my experience we're apt to be most successful if we don't try to force our belief on others. If we wait until we're asked, we can be sure the other person is at least curious about our philosophy. And we can be sure we *will* be asked if, instead of apologizing for our faith, we show in our daily lives that we have something extra special to be happy about.

When we *are* asked it's wise not to do too much "mouth witnessing" without enough "ear listening." It helps to know what the other person is thinking, especially the one who might be antireligious. If we listen, after we've heard all the negatives, we can then wipe them out with a good positive statement. We should encourage questions, let the questions be asked before we supply all the answers in a flood of what to them may seem like verbal nonsense. Be sensitive to the other's feelings and thoughts even if they're totally different from our own. Be sincere and honest. Admit the things you don't know and can't answer. This will only bring respect. If you always use the first person this can't be questioned. "I've found the philosophy that works for *me,* and I wish you could have it, too. But I don't want to push."

If we've actually got that special something, they'll want it, and keep digging until they uncover our philosophy. Then it's something they've gotten through their own desire and efforts and they'll value it.

On the other hand, when we're asked to address our church or a young people's group, or to give a public testimony to our faith, we have to channel our enthusiasm into a few effective, concise statements that says it all as far as we're concerned. If we're not prepared to do this our witness is confused and confusing. True, with God's help, I've heard some beautiful, spontaneous testimonies burst out of confusion. I remember a little boy who got so mixed up the first time he tried to give public expression to his faith that he gave up after some agonized false starts and much squirming. "The only way I can say it," he informed us, "is that being a Christian is like eating a Peter Paul Almond Joy. It's indescribably delicious!"

But for myself I've found that, while moments of spontaneous inspiration do come, God can do so much more through us if we're not only a willing but a *ready* vessel. Telling others of our philosophy of life should be the most important speech we'll ever make, regardless of the size of the listening audience or the place where it is presented. The reason is obvious. We will be in a position to say something that may have a lasting effect on someone there. What we present may call forth a response from someone in the audience far more important than applause, a response that could mean a changed life. We'll be privileged to be the one who can introduce Christ Himself. So our selection of words, our understanding of what we ourselves believe, and the way in which we present our thoughts are of the utmost importance.

Here, more than ever, we need to do our homework of *planning,* to *prepare* in every way we can, to *pray* for the extra help we need. Even if it's just a chance to speak briefly, we take it, remembering that by holding a *positive picture* by accepting the possibility of a few miracles, with His help they just might happen.

As we learn to pray effectively by praying, so we learn to give an effective witness by witnessing. If we do the very best we can each time we're asked, we'll find better and better ways to present our beliefs. But perhaps I can help you shorten the learning process if I share with you a few rules that experience has taught me.

Keep it simple . . . from the heart.

I gave my first big public testimony before the largest audience I had ever faced on my own campus at Arizona State. I had already won the Miss Arizona title and, since I really wanted it to be used of God, when a member of the Billy Graham team asked me to give a three-minute personal witness before the students at a Graham crusade, I said an enthusiastic yes. I prepared carefully with a basic outline—how, when, and why I found a need for Christ and asked Him to become a real part of my life—What made my faith important to me—What could make it important to others like myself. Then I worked out my notes and clipped them in my Bible.

It wasn't until the services began and I was face to face with that huge crowd, including girls from my dorm, kids I went to class with, and hundreds of strangers who might know nothing about Christianity, that I realized that, while my outline was right, my whole approach was wrong. It was too intellectual, the words too neatly arranged, too complicated, far too complicated for such an easy subject. It was a well-planned little speech that didn't say it at all like I felt it. In a flash I knew that an effective witness had to come from the heart as well as the head. But getting that flash at the last moment threw me into a confusion worse than stage fright. At this point, you pray. I did. I said something like this:

"Lord, You know how important this is to me, but I want it to be important for You. Please help me to express myself and the way I feel inside in such a way that the people here will somehow understand what You can be to them, if they will just let You! I know what I should say, just help me to say it. Thank You. Amen."

Come to think of it I don't believe I closed with "Amen." I think the prayer was left with an open end just in case I needed to add an extra "help!" My prayer was answered that night and I was asked to go to San Diego to be on a national telecast with the Billy Graham Crusade. They wanted me to say just what I'd said on campus. When they handed me a copy of that first testimony it timed out to three minutes on the nose and said exactly what I had hoped it would.

Say it in your own words . . . be natural.

During my Miss America year, as I had many opportunities to give a public witness, I looked for new ways to improve my presentation. Relating experiences as Miss America was easy, and they had their points, but I discovered that wearing a crown, even a temporary one, sometimes set me and my experiences a little apart. So I tried to get even closer to my audiences. I worked at sounding organized, but unrehearsed, almost ad-lib in my talks. This resulted in a conversational approach which helped establish a rapport. I was saying everything as naturally, as undramatically as possible using the same words and expressions I would use if I was talking to one individual.

If you have time, make use of stories other than your own.

After my reign, when I continued making appearances at churches of all denominations, at Youth for Christ rallies, and on Campus Crusade programs, I found my allotted time running longer. After I gave my personal testimony I would tell of the many excited teen-agers I had met who had shared with me why they thought Christ was so important to them. This was a helpful addition because, if there were youngsters in the audience who still envisioned me up on a throne, they could identify with these others whose lives so closely resembled their own.

Use Scripture positively, then present God's plan.

Talking with various young people I found some turned off about religion because they had been approached negatively—with Bible threats about death and hell. Even if they were true these youngsters refused to be frightened into heaven, so the importance of using positive quotes from Scripture in my testimony grew. Christ's actual words of *hope* and *cheer* and *love* were so much more effective than my own, and of much greater importance. I have been thrilled to see so many young people turn-on to Christ out of desire instead of fear.

Eternity is certainly longer and, in the end, far more important than a mere lifetime. But the Now generation wants to know, "What's in it for me *now?*" There's a lot, so why not tell them? This is what I like to say: "Christ can become your Friend, that Friend who 'sticketh closer than a brother,' as the Bible puts it. He is always ready to listen to your prayers, to answer them, to help you with your problems big and small. He can keep us happy, full of peace, and really overflowing with hope. He can provide a philosophy that really works, that gives us a strong foundation that nothing can shake or destroy. These are just a few of His gifts and these gifts He offers us for life *now*."

Then I can tell them how God crowned His perfect plan. It was Billy Zeoli who said to me, "Vonda, if you present God's plan to man (that Christ came into the world, died on the cross, rose from the dead, so that we could have eternal life), Scripture has promised your words will be honored." He warned me not to say it indirectly, but boldly, and specifically as it happened. And I have found that when I do state it this way that promise is kept.

Next time you are asked to give a testimony (and if you're not asked, why not volunteer?) remember first how important what you have to say can be to the people listening. Open your communication lines with the key: think about them and you'll forget about yourself. Know what you want to say, then keep it simple. Say it in your own words, from your heart. Don't be general and just talk about God. Tell them it is Christ who gives you the reality of your faith and it is through Him that we can have companionship with God. Let others know the difference your faith has made in your life and why you recommend it to them. In other words, be positive. Use Christ's own words to express His love. If you have time, make use of the lives and statements of others to show how all-embracing His love is. Explain how easy it is to become a Christian, and what an exciting, full life a person can have by simply accepting Him. Tell them this life extends into eternity.

Have your *purpose* firmly in mind: to win others to Christ. *Plan* and *prepare:* devote time, energy and thought to what you are going to share. *Pray* for help and inspiration from above. Make sure your presentation is honest, straightforward, relying on your sincerity and fact rather than emotionalism.

Like those early Christians you, too, can be a winner, a winner of "souls," if your testimony states clearly the Great News that *"Happiness is knowing the Lord!"*

12

Reach Up!

I've never been able to agree with Juliet that "parting is such sweet sorrow." In fact I can't bring myself to say a negative farewell. When my good friends and I have to part we say positively, "See ya!"

You and I are now good friends. Together in these pages we've held a mirror up to life, life as it really is with all its beauty, its exciting challenges, its great opportunities, and its equally difficult problems. We've talked as good friends do about happiness, and what it is; about success, and how to achieve it; about your unique talents and personality, and how to make the most of them. We've discussed men and marriage, women and careers; your present and your future; self-confidence, goals, character. We've covered the great, wide, wonderful world, and dummies, philosophy, the moon, and cherry sodas with chocolate ice cream.

Because you are my friends, because I want you to be that special person I think God wants each one of us to become, free to love and create and experience and enjoy, I've tried to share my thoughts with you exactly as I would if we could get together in my living room for a rap session.

So instead of saying good-bye now, let's say what we'd say at my front door, "See ya!" and hope it will be soon. But I wouldn't want you to leave without a parting gift. So here is one of the

first songs I ever wrote. I wrote it *for* you, and when I sing it,
I sing it *to* you. It's called "Reach Up," and it's meant to offer
the very best I have to share.

> Reach up for the new life,
>   Filled with the greatest love.
> Reach up for the real life,
>   By trusting in God above.
> Open up your heart to Him,
>   Follow in His perfect way,
> And you will find the dawning
>   Of a newer, brighter day.
> He offers you a lasting peace,
>   An answer to every prayer.
> Just look up to the heavens and
>   You'll find Him waiting there.
> Reach up for the good life,
>   It waits for you and me,
> Reach up for the best life,
>   Have faith and believe.

If you reach up then you, too, will find you'll never step
down. Each new year you'll be moving forward—
> *"to a new life,*
>   *a new challenge,"*
>   *a greater happiness!*